The Compact House Book

The Compact House Book

SECOND EDITION

Edited by Don Metz

A Garden Way Publishing Book

 Storey Communications, Inc.
Pownal, Vermont 05261

**Printed in the United States by W.A. Krueger Co.
Second printing, July 1989**

**Library of Congress Cataloging in
Publication Data**

Main entry under title:

The Compact house book.

  1. Small houses - United States - Designs and
plans. 2. Small houses - United States - Awards. 3.
Architect-designed houses - United States-
Designs and plans.
I. Metz, Don.
NA7205.C65 1983   728.3'7'0223   83-8912
ISBN 0-88266-323-2 (paperback)
ISBN 0-88266-351-8 (hardcover)

Contents

Introduction

The problem has been the same for decades: affordable housing that is inexpensive to maintain, to heat, and to cool. But more than that, housing that is imaginative and enjoyable.

The problem gnawed at the brain of Don Metz, a New England architect whose creative structures grace the finest communities, and whose underground homes injected new ways of thinking into the plans of his fellow architects.

There was some way, he was sure, that the dreams of many for inspiring housing could be meshed with the gritty problems of financing.

His first move was to Vermont and Garden Way Publishing. There he met with editorial and marketing groups. It was a January day, clear and cold, a day that steered any thoughts of affordable heating toward something better than turning down the thermostat and putting on more clothing.

Metz explained his aim, then ideas were tossed out, scrutinized, and rejected. There was agreement on one thing: Metz and this group should be able to contribute something that would mitigate the problem of affordable housing.

Perhaps the thinking took a turn when Metz explained the link between the square footage of a house and the size of payments the bank would expect each month. Perhaps that was when compact housing was first mentioned. It seemed ideal for many — today's smaller families, the elderly, singles who preferred living alone.

The idea grew. Get the ideas of many . . . from across the country . . . those facing heat problems as well as the cold . . . but how? Ask for contributions? Hire architects? What about a contest, with the winners' entries in the book?

There was instant agreement. Then Metz guided the group through decisions on what the compact home would be. The floor plan would be limited to 1,000 square feet. It would include two bedrooms, a bath, storage space, and combination living-dining-kitchen facilities. Emphasis on practicality, energy-efficiency, and aesthetic integrity were defined as key ingredients. Contestants would be asked to furnish typical construction details for the reader.

An announcement of the contest brought a flurry of some 2,200 inquiries to Garden Way Publishing. By the November 1 deadline, 421 bulky packages — the entries — had taken over the office of one Garden Way Publishing editor.

Metz looked over a sample of the entries. His conclusion: They were first class and merited a first-class panel of judges to select the winners.

He chose carefully: Canadian architect John Hix for his valuable perspectives on cold-climate design. The peripatetic Barry Berkus of California for his architectural experience in all levels of housing production. Architect and author Don Watson for his leadership role in solar design. Ralph Johnson, president of the National Association of Home Builders, for his years of experience in the marketplace and his steadying influence on the architect-jurors' inclination toward the fanciful. As director of the competition and a practitioner in the field of energy-efficient design, Metz was agreed upon as jury foreman.

After preliminary sessions reduced the number of entries to be judged to 100, the judges met in the spacious offices of the National Association of Home Builders in Washington, D.C., where the entries could be spread out on a horseshoe-shaped table of impressive dimensions.

The judges quickly ran over the entries, expressed surprise at their high quality, then plunged in — studying, comparing, discussing, taking notes. Eight hours later they reached their conclusions, naming the winners and the others that would be included in the book.

Metz was satisfied that the goals of the contest had been reached. "The projects chosen fulfill the needs of a wide variety of tastes, budgets, and climatic conditions," he said. "They range from the practical to the exotic. They all share to some degree an efficient use of space, aesthetic appeal, and energy-wise detailing."

This book offers readers an opportunity to agree or disagree with Metz and the judges. More than that, it offers them an opportunity to enjoy compact housing by selecting a favorite design, then beginning work on it with their architects or home contractors.

Readers not looking for new housing will find another use for this book. By studying the plans and other drawings, they will discover valuable ideas for storage space, passive solar heating, ways to build privacy into small homes — the list goes on and on.

As this, the second edition of the book goes to press, we at Garden Way Publishing have added confidence to the early enthusiasm felt by Metz and those who created this book.

We have talked with people who have built these houses. We have seen their smiles, their pride as they have shown their homes to us. We are confident that this book will help those who long for affordable, enjoyable homes.

Site Plan

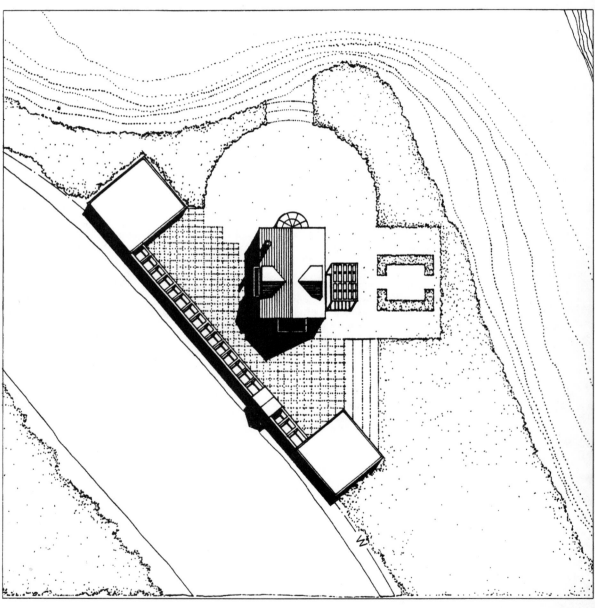

This is a very buildable design. Its simplicity is a plus.
Ralph Johnson, judge

It is classic in tradition, and its focal point, the bay window, is a classic collonade. It draws your eye to that back wall. I see myself sitting in that bay.
Barry Berkus, judge

This house uses formal, classical elements. There are a lot of ideas here.
John Hix, judge

A very cerebral plan. So simple and subtle with elegant proportions.
Don Metz, judge

Temple

**Designer:
Lee B. Temple**

This design sums up the aims of the compact house design competition, proving that a house of 1,000 or fewer square feet can be beautiful, a place to enjoy living, a model of simplicity.

There's more than a hint of the religious in this house, with its basilica shape, its transept for living space, its dramatic two-story apse.

Practicality, too, is built into the design, with multiplicity of function in the rooms, and passive solar heating promising warmth at bargain rates.

The simplicity of the design is what led the judges to declare this the best of the entries.

By Lee B. Temple

Situation
A small, triangular, wooded bluff overlooks Cayuga Lake, shoehorned between Frontenac Road on the north and the 200-foot Frontenac Gorge and Falls to the south, eleven miles northwest of Ithaca, New York. We must draw out certain qualities from the site in order to create a place of retreat for a professional couple whose priorities include simplicity, practicality, and meditation.

Site Strategy
Here we chose to collage two typical forms: garden wall and sacred object building. Due to the tight, delicate site conditions, we kept the house modestly scaled, and placed the non-heated services against the wall. This provides a buffer to road noise and cold northern winds, and serves as a backdrop/foreground to the chapel, through containment of the outbuilding functions: potting shed, entry portal, wood storage loggia, and carport. It is deformed to accept changes in elevation and function.

The object building contains living accommodation, and heightens the contemplative introversion fostered by the wall, cliff edge, and woods. Each side of the pure volume is uniquely deformed due to internal considerations, and to focus on a particular aspect of its relation to landscape and wall: the wooden porch accepts entry courtyard; the wooden kitchen saddlebag addresses wall and evening sitting terrace; the glass dining area and bedroom dormer open southward to the garden; and the glass apse finds culmination in the distant view.

Relation
We have outlined a method of problem solution which addresses universal architectural issues, such as: the role of history and context as typological language, the potential flexibility, economy, and range of spatial qualities derived from differentiation of building systems, as values in our time; and we have demonstrated ease of implementation in a variety of situations. As an example, this modest house of 1,000 square feet is compact—a small, efficient structure

**Technical Data
Project**
Chapelle Frontenac
Gross square feet
1,000
Location
Covert, New York
7,000 degree days
Elevation, 480 feet

Major order
Load-bearing block, walls with stuccoed exterior insulation on concrete footings, tile over insulated slab on grade, 4 × 10 insulated industrial wood roof, three-foot-square double glazing
Minor order
Wood posts support wooden joist floors, ve-

neered plywood cabinetry and interior facades, oak stairs, wooden kitchen saddlebag, entry porch, and bedroom dormer, glass apse. Bricolage materials incorporated where available
Type
Hybrid insulated/solar warm/cool zone concept. Heat retaining slab, insulated masonry walls,

wood stove, hot water baseboard (back-up), natural ventilation providing good space for an affordable price, reestablishing architecture as place-making of eternal presence within the realm of everyone.

Building Strategy
The dichotomous building is composed of two complementary orders, denoting the union of inner and outer forces. The major order adopts a standard building typology (chosen archetype) as social role: the volume, scaffold, orientation. The minor order, within or attached to the major order, manifests personal necessities unique to the individual: the interior space, exhibit, identification. In this case, the major order (masonry shell) reinterprets the votive chapel as protected enclave; the minor order (wood fill and attachments) turns further inward with strongly articulated rooms each with a particular quality augmented by natural light. The sacral imagery is intended here to emphasize the spirit of the place.

Potential
Flexibility of the concepts governing this house may be demonstrated in the accommodation of growth over time in relation to owner need, and in the ability of the basic kit of parts to adapt to a variety of typical housing situations. Rooms assume multiplicity of function (living/guest, bed/library/den, etc.). Relations between major and minor order may vary from conjunction to opposition, and buildings may adapt to urban (1), rural (2), flat (3), or hilly (4) situations, assume appropriate volumetric images (i.e., brownstone, barn, tower, or temple) and internal programs (basilica, free plan, front/back, servant/served, etc.).

Construction Strategy
Concern for energy efficiency in the development of the dichotomous building demonstrates the potential of cross-breeding principles of superinsulation and passive solar design.

The volume (major order) is insulated on the outside to provide thermal mass on the inside. The interior (minor order) is in this case layered into three heating zones. Areas of cooler temperature (living room, entry, baths, and stairs) provide an air lock for areas of warmer temperature (kitchen, dining room, bedrooms). Zoning differentiation is reinforced by method of heating: cool zones have thermal mass in insulated walls, augmented by wood stove (living room) and baseboard (baths), or are left unheated (entry and stairs). The warm zone becomes a kind of kernel due to the air lock provided by cool zones, and has solar access to a heat-retaining slab (slab on grade and tiles over joists upstairs), as well as physical closure (wood infill, operable doors and shutters) from cool zones for necessary temperature modulation.

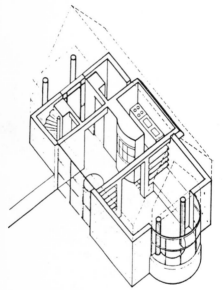 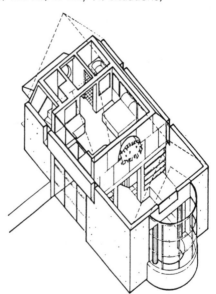 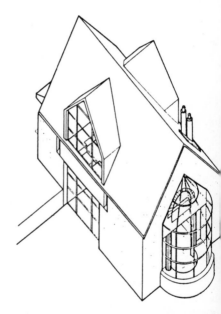

Perspectives

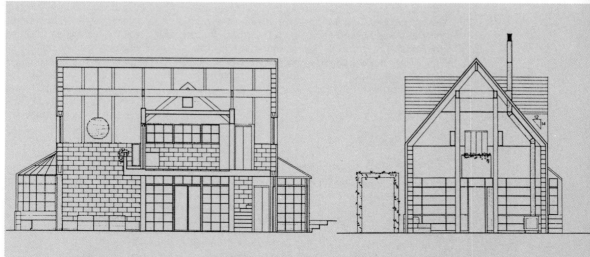

Elevations

Wall Section

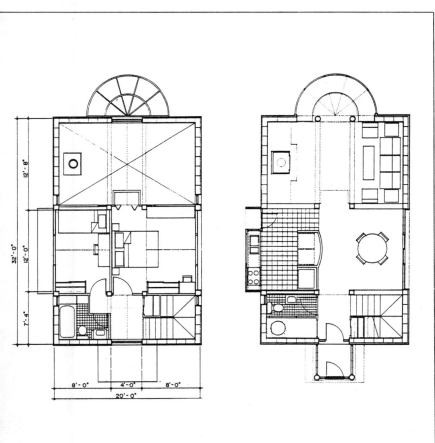

Floor Plan

1-Typical Roof Construction
Asphalt shingles over ½"
plywood over 4" foam and
2 × 4 sleepers over vapor
barrier over 8" fiberglass
and 4 × 10 rafters over ½"
plywood R = 32

2-Typical Wall Construction
½" stucco over metal
lathe attached to 8" CMU
thru 4" rigid foam
insulation and vapor
barrier R = 24
¾" Pressure Treated
board over 4" rigid foam
insulation over vapor
barrier over 8" CMU

3-Typical Floor Construction
6" conc. slab on grade
over vapor barrier over 5"
gravel

4-Typical Foundation
1' × 2' conc. footing
poured in place w/rein-
forcing bars, 4" drain tile

Perspective

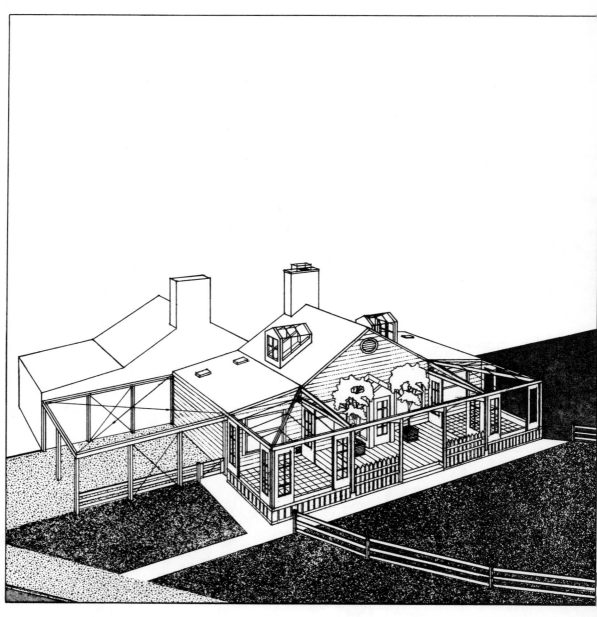

A simple approach that pulls it off.
Don Watson, judge

The separation of beds around the core allows a lot of flexibility for the lifestyle of the dweller. This is a direct solution for the problems of a small house. The kitchen being dark could be a problem.
Barry Berkus, judge

It addresses the concept of semi-detached housing. Its simplicity is very appealing.
John Hix, judge

A good, solid plan.
Don Metz, judge

Parts of the patio convert into multi-exposure solar greenhouses for passive solar design.
David Leash, architect

David Leash

Compact house planning poses a myriad of problems. And more are added when the compact house is part of a cluster development.

Lack of privacy, a boxed-in feeling, monotony—these are only some of the troubles that often are a part of a development.

David Leash, in this award-winning design, has recognized, confronted, and offered solutions to these troubles.

The units are in groups of eight, with shared common ground, plus the privacy of individual patios. These clusters avoid the monotony of single-family houses,

each facing the street. Windows are carefully placed to provide sunlight and views—and privacy as well. The windows plus an interior sloped roof combine to avoid the closed-in feel of many compact house designs. So too does the broad patio, visible from all of the living-dining area.

There are things that work well in this design—the separation of two sleeping areas; the luxury, in compact homes, of two baths; the convenience of the laundry; and the open living area. Cabin fever won't threaten dwellers here.

By David Leash

Project Assumption
To provide an affordable compact house for middle-income buyers in a suburban housing development.

Approaches
Increased density to reduce cost of land per dwelling.

Use of mini-clusters to give more visual interest and mass to small units. Common open space created and number of curb cuts minimized.

Strongly defined streetscape created by assembling mini-clusters in manner to avoid monotonous rows of small detached units common to many subdivisions.

Architectural design based on most desired housing vernacular determined by market surveys.

Plan simplified but variation of space provided. Bedroom-bath areas separated for guests or shared use of home.

Maximum use of insulated exterior walls and roof for energy conservation.

Use of conventional wood construction.

Group-maintained, drought-free landscaping to reduce maintenance work for owners.

Owner-maintained patio provided at each unit.

Special Features and Advantages
Site is well drained non-agricultural land in area occupied by single-family dwellings.

Site has little initial visual interest. Landscaping, mounding, and street pattern are used to enhance views and create sheltered areas.

Higher sloping roof pitch over living areas and vent allow escape of warm air in summer. Heat recycled in winter by fan and duct from ceiling to floor at living area.

Parts of patio convert into multi-exposure solar greenhouses for passive solar design.

Technical Data
Project
Compact House
Gross square feet
1,000
Location
Redwood City, California
2,596 degree days
Elevation, 31 feet

Materials
Wood framing and siding, gypsum board interior, wood trim
Type
Energy conservation to meet California Title 24, passive solar

Floor Plan

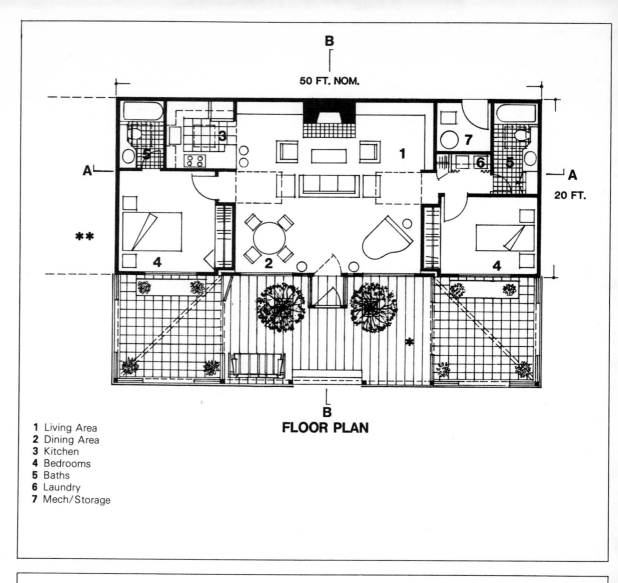

B

50 FT. NOM.

A

A

20 FT.

**

1 Living Area
2 Dining Area
3 Kitchen
4 Bedrooms
5 Baths
6 Laundry
7 Mech/Storage

B

FLOOR PLAN

Site Plan

Solar Orientation:
Southeast facing unit il-
lustrated. House designed to
adapt to multiple exposures
of the site plan, as typical
for grouped housing.

Site Conditions:
Utilities:
Underground utilities
Weather:
Moderate, Dry Mar-Nov,
Rainy Season Nov-Mar
Landscaping:
For Wind Control, Street
Definition and Privacy.
3 ft. high fencing to define
Mini-Clusters.
Roof Pitches:
1.5:12, 7.5:12

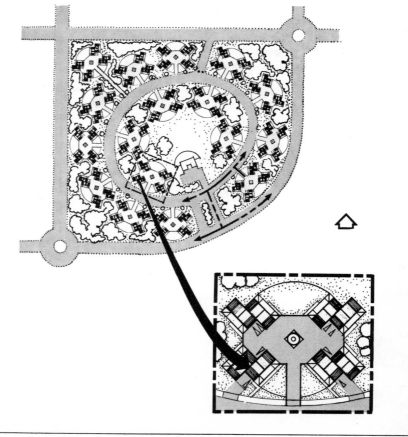

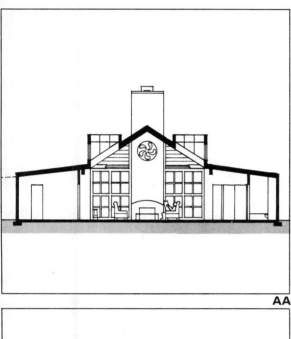

AA

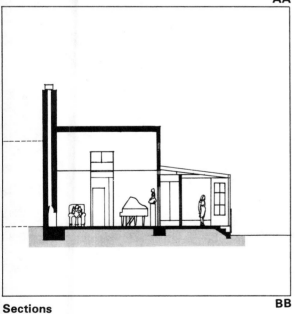

Sections

BB

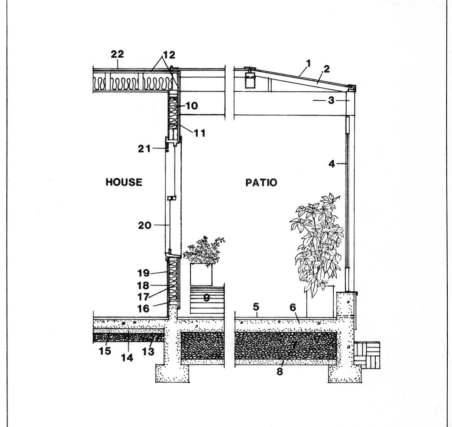

Wall Section

HOUSE   PATIO

1-Tempered Glass
2-Anodized Alum.
3-Timber Framing
4-Wood/Glass Doors
5-Tile
6-Conc. Slab
7-Rock Thermal Storage
8-Pumice
9-Water Thermal Storage
10-Vent Beyond
11-Wood Siding
12-Plywood Sheathing

13-Gravel
14-Sand
15-Vapor Barrier
16-Wood Framing
17-Insulation
18-Vapor Barrier
19-Gypsum Board Interior
20-Operable Sash
21-Adjustable Louver
22-Roofing

9

Axonometric

The impact on entering this house is very strong. The greenhouse is attractive. Nice things are happening here.
Barry Berkus, judge

A good solution for a south-facing slope with good use of the greenhouse.
Don Metz, judge

The upper floor could over-heat from the western sun hitting the stairwell. It's a very dramatic design.
John Hix, judge

The house is composed of terraces oriented due south to capture the spectacular view (of the California coast) and maximize the mild climate.
Nancy Scheinholtz, designer

Scheinholtz

Nancy Scheinholtz

This house, compared with others in the book, is expensive.

It's also well planned for its setting — northern California, and a lot that slopes to the south and faces the Pacific Ocean.

The house is ideal for a sunny location, with its two-story greenhouse, two huge decks, vast areas of glass, passive solar heating, and solar collector panels to provide the domestic hot water.

Because of the slope of the site, entrance to this house is on the upper level, from a deck and leading to the dining room, but handy to the kitchen. The living room is thus protected from traffic.

The lower level features a bath, greenhouse, bedroom/study, and a master bedroom accessible only through the greenhouse.

Planners should note that this house is larger than the others because the designer chose not to consider the greenhouse as living space. This greenhouse, linked with the dining room on the second floor, joins with the glassed stairway to provide a sense of spaciousness not expected in a house of this size.

As you can see from the wall section illustration, most of the glass area is shaded from unwanted summer sunshine, but is receptive to the heat of winter sunshine.

By Nancy Scheinholtz

This site is located in the hills above the rugged California coast. The house is composed of terraces oriented due south to capture the spectacular view and maximize the mild climate. The architectural form of the house is generated by the northern California vernacular combined with passive solar access needs.

The minimum heating requirements of the house are served on the lower level by a greenhouse which collects heat and radiates it through the thermal mass of the floor slab.

The upper level is also heated by the greenhouse in combination with the fireplace. In addition, there is a small auxiliary mechanical system if poor weather conditions persist.

Technical Data
Project
Muir Beach Compact House
Gross square feet
990, excluding terraces and greenhouse
Location
Marin County, California
3,000 degree days
Elevation, near sea level

Materials
Wood frame construction, redwood siding and decks, aluminum details
Type
Passive solar heating, solar collector panels for domestic hot water supply

11

Site Plan

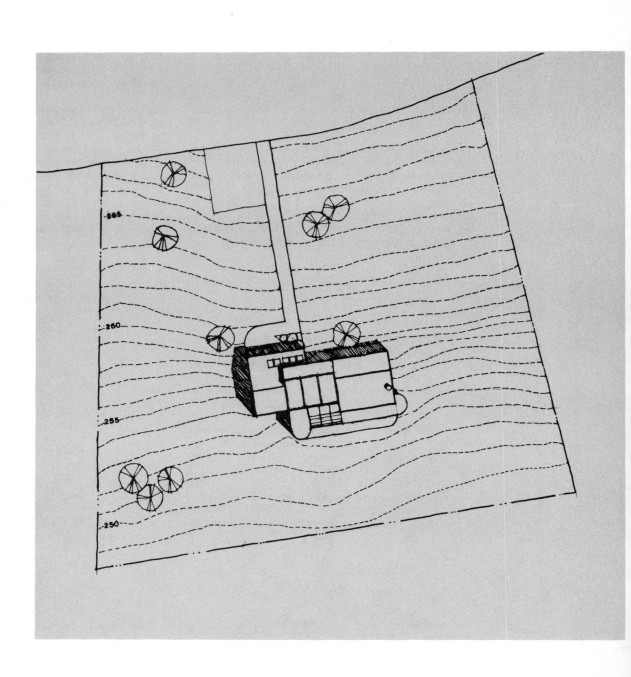

Upper Level Plan

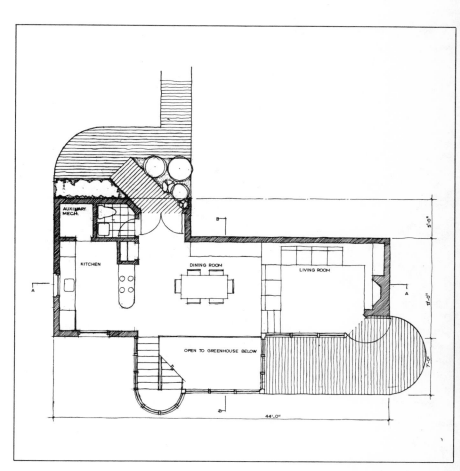

Lower Level Plan

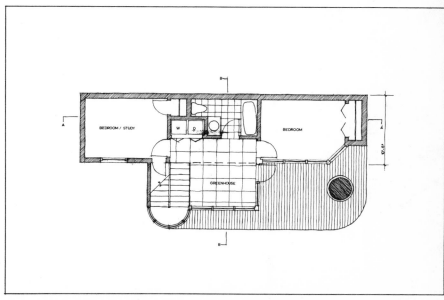

Section AA

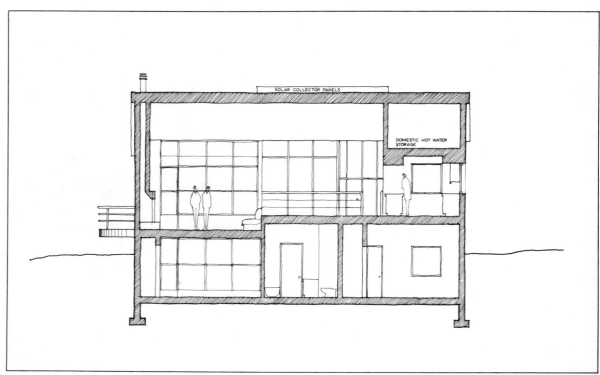

Section BB

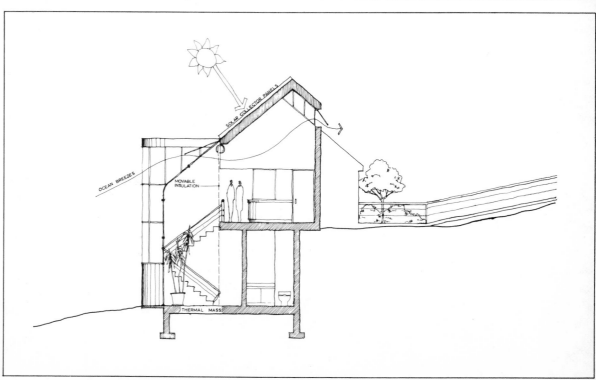

Wall Section

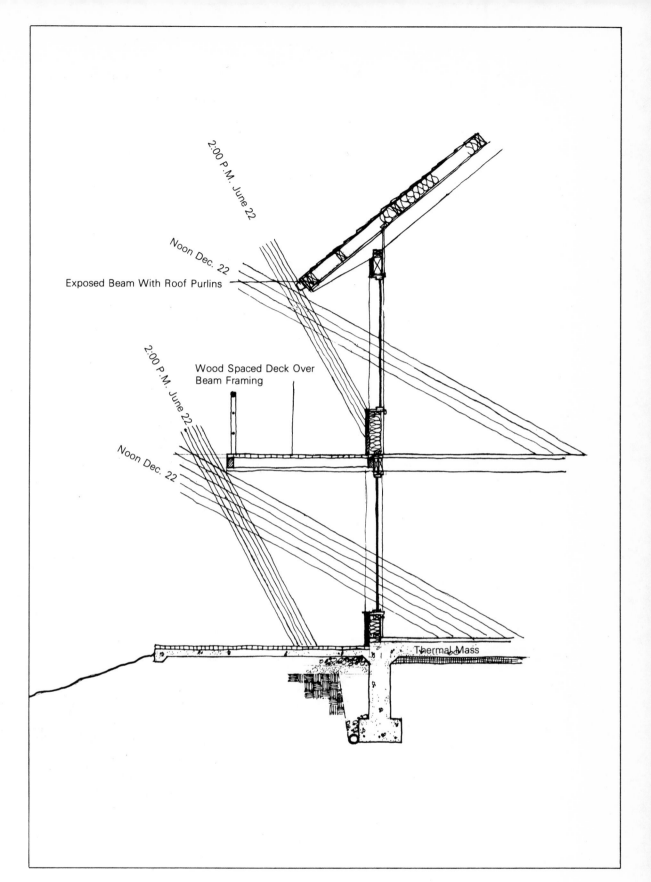

2:00 P.M. June 22

Noon Dec. 22

Exposed Beam With Roof Purlins

Wood Spaced Deck Over
Beam Framing

2:00 P.M. June 22

Noon Dec. 22

Thermal Mass

Elevation

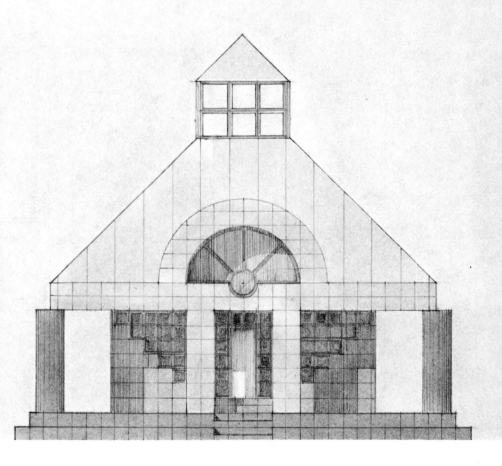

The analysis of the formal elements is among the best of the entries. The plan elements are skewed and add variety to a classic composition. The overall composition is balanced and gives a sense of a well-defined place.
Don Watson, judge

The overscaled elements evoke a variety of allusions to historical architectural vocabularies from the classical to Art Deco.
Don Metz, judge

It is based on the traditional southern house type, with a wide roof overhang for maximum shading.
Gordon Ashworth, designer

Ashworth

Gordon Ashworth

This house will fit the needs of a small family in a warm climate. It features a wide roof that serves a double role, shading and making this house appear to be much larger than it really is.

By Gordon Ashworth

This entry is a proposal for a small house on a sub-urban subdivision on the outskirts of Gainesville, Florida.

It is designed in the belief that it is possible to build a small, formal house which combines many of the advantages of compact planning and energy-efficient design with the usual functional and psychological needs of a small, middle-class, suburban family.

It is based on the traditional southern house type, with a wide roof overhang for maximum shading. It is freestanding and set on a plinth above ground. A series of vents at ground level bring air into the house and circulate it vertically through a thermal chimney.

The design attempts to solve the problem of size by using a big roof to give the impression of largeness, and overscaled elements, such as the entrance dormer and columns.

Technical Data
Project
Classical Florida House
Gross square feet
1,000
Location
Gainesville, Florida
Elevation, 75 feet

Materials
Concrete block, stud frame, corrugated metal, ceramic tile
Type
Traditional, naturally ventilated, active solar potential

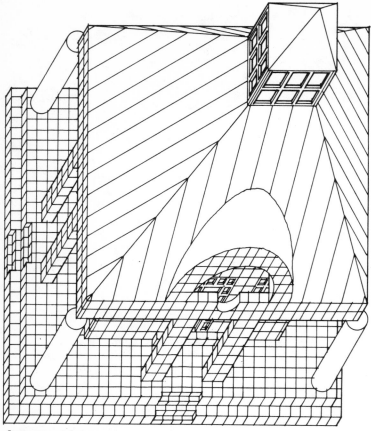

Axonometric

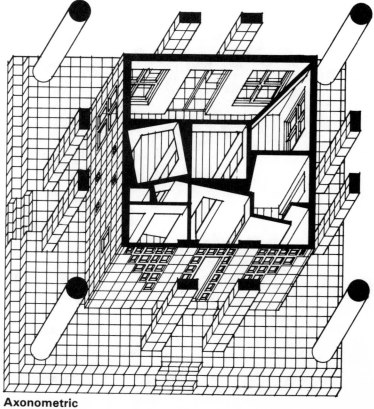

Axonometric

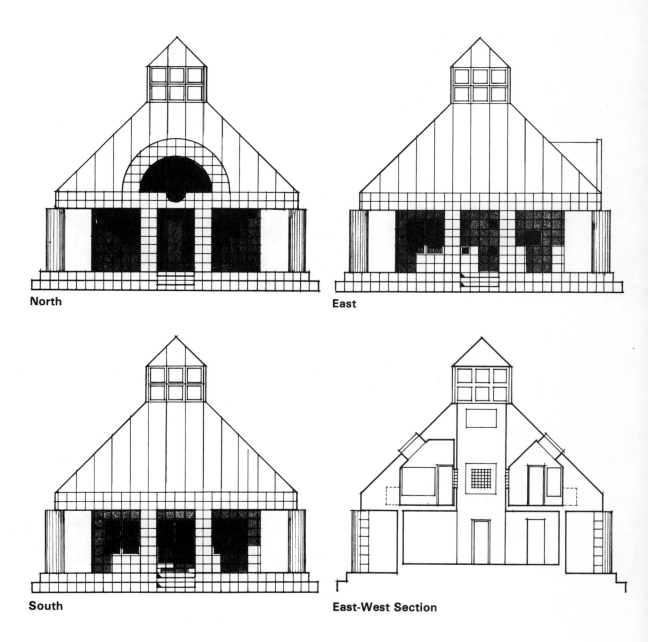

North

East

South

East-West Section

19

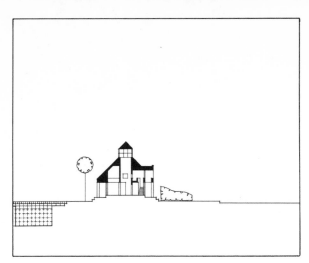

Site Plan

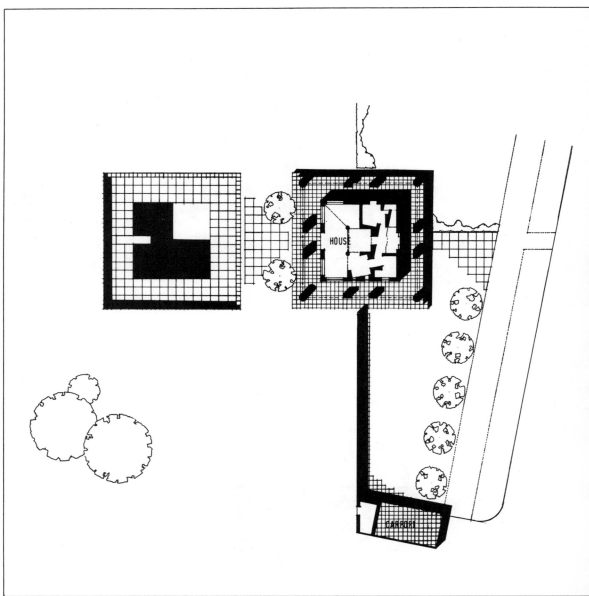

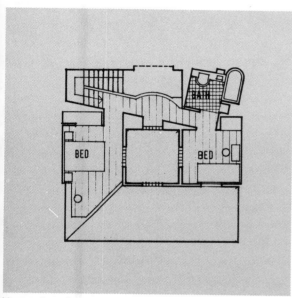

Upper Level

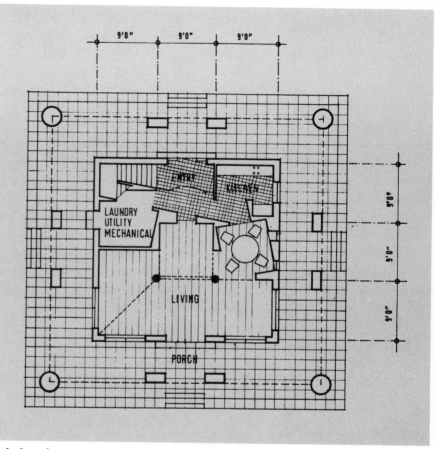

Main Level

21

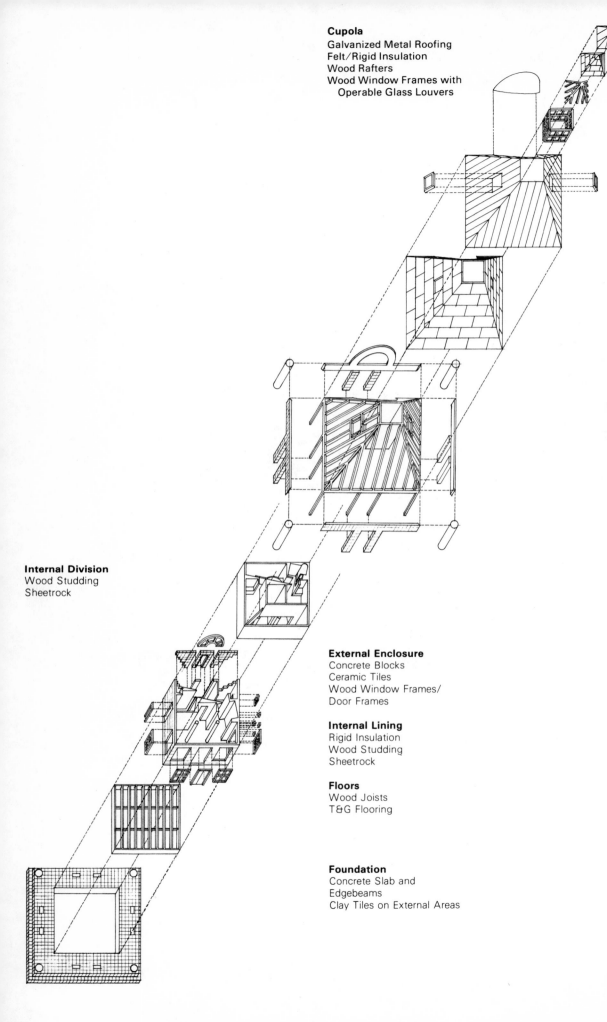

Cupola
Galvanized Metal Roofing
Felt/Rigid Insulation
Wood Rafters
Wood Window Frames with
   Operable Glass Louvers

Roof
Galvanized Metal Roofing
Felt/Rigid Insulation
Wood Rafters/Corner
   Beams/Edge Beams
Metal Skylights

Structure
Tubular Steel Columns
Steel Angle Beams
(All Faced with
Wood Studding, Plywood
and Tiles; Except Corner
Columns Which Are
Faced with Circular Glass
Fibre casings)

Internal Division
Wood Studding
Sheetrock

External Enclosure
Concrete Blocks
Ceramic Tiles
Wood Window Frames/
Door Frames

Internal Lining
Rigid Insulation
Wood Studding
Sheetrock

Floors
Wood Joists
T&G Flooring

Foundation
Concrete Slab and
Edgebeams
Clay Tiles on External Areas

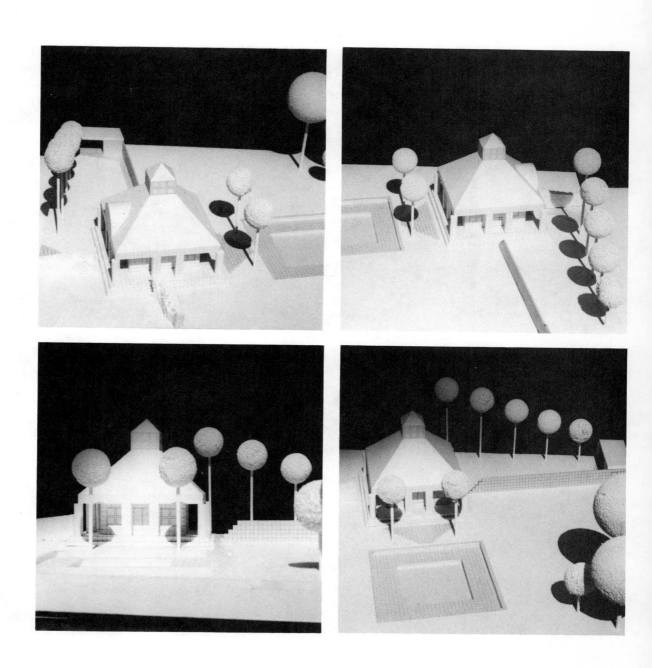

Perspective

Plain Jane—but nice.
Don Watson, judge

The basic house can
accommodate changing
family patterns.
Linda Brock, designer

Brock

Linda Brock
Energy consultant:
Russ Heliker

The designer has thought beyond the immediate needs of her client to the lifetime span of that client's family. The result is a home that promises comfort and convenience in a variety of situations, from a growing family to retirement years.

Add to that the advantages of energy efficiency and an open plan, and you have a house design suitable for many geographical areas and family lifestyles.

Unique in this design is the opportunity it offers to create a third bedroom.

By Linda Brock

The basic house can accommodate changing family patterns. A single person or couple builds the house, utilizing the upper level as a master bedroom and the entire lower level as a "Great Room" by omitting the closet between the kitchen and the lower bedroom area.

Later the lower bedroom space could become an office with easy accessibility to the front door.

When children arrive, the master bedroom moves downstairs. If additional space is required, another bedroom on the upper level can be provided simply by installing floor decking over the living room.

This can be removed at a later date to regain the spacial variation on the lower level. As the couple grow older, the master bedroom remains on the lower level so they can avoid climbing the stairs daily, and the upper level is used as guest quarters.

The basic house is energy-efficient and cost-effective in its massing. Optimal framing is employed with the 2 × 6 studs at twenty-four inches on center for the first floor framing, and by minimizing the number of walls.

With the exception of the patio glass doors, no glazing interrupts the bearing wall framing.

The prefabricated truss forms the floor, side walls, ceiling, and roof of the upper level. (I have used a similar truss on low-cost housing and found it to be very cost-effective.)

Sixty-eight percent of the glazing is on the south side, with an inexpensive slab on grade for solar storage.

Major living areas are on the south side. Because winter winds are from the north and west, penetrations in these walls are kept to a minimum.

Technical Data
Project
Cost-effective Compact House
Gross square feet
1,000
Location
Bozeman, Montana
8,100 degree days
Elevation, 4,850 feet

Materials
2 × 6 wooden studs with 10/12 pitch wood truss
Type
Energy-efficient, well insulated, passive solar

The insulation is R-26 in the walls and R-50 in the ceiling to match projected energy costs. Air infiltration is limited to one-half air change per hour. With the occasional use of the back-up electric radiant heat, the house is heated with two cords of wood a year.

Optional additions shown include vestibules at the front and garden entries, and a two-car garage with space for wood storage. Other options could be a full basement on a south-sloping lot, and cedar or redwood siding for lower maintenance costs. The basic house meets all requirements of the Uniform Building Code and FHA minimum property standards.

Site Plan

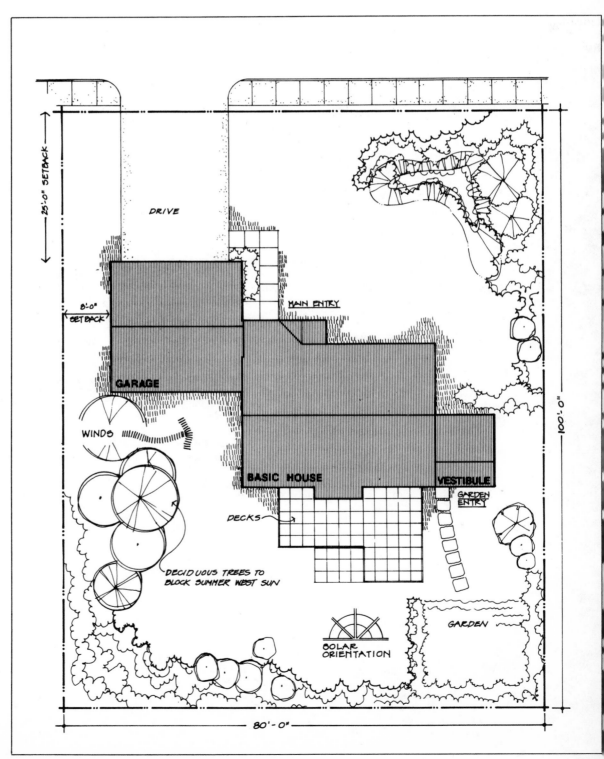

Floor Plan

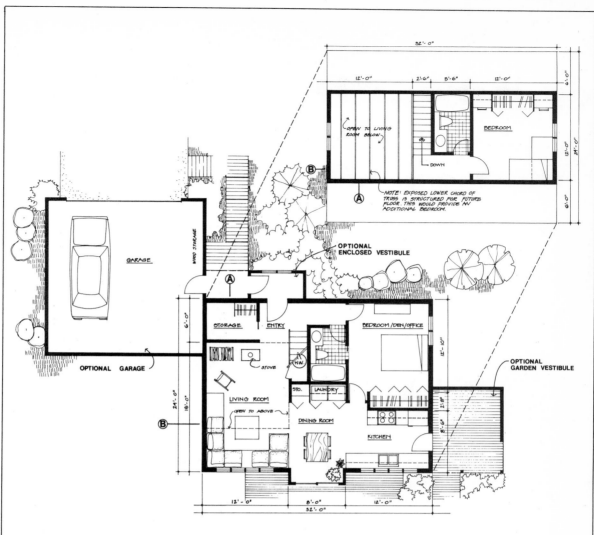

32'-0"
12'-0" 2'-6" 5'-6" 12'-0"
6'-0"

OPEN TO LIVING ROOM BELOW

BEDROOM

DOWN

24'-0"
12'-0"

6'-0"

NOTE: EXPOSED LOWER CHORD OF TRUSS IS STRUCTURED FOR FUTURE FLOOR. THIS WOULD PROVIDE AN ADDITIONAL BEDROOM.

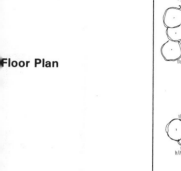

GARAGE

WOOD STORAGE

OPTIONAL ENCLOSED VESTIBULE

OPTIONAL GARDEN VESTIBULE

STORAGE   ENTRY

BEDROOM /DEN/OFFICE

OPTIONAL GARAGE

STOVE

H.W.

STO.   LAUNDRY

12'-10"

LIVING ROOM

OPEN TO ABOVE

DINING ROOM

KITCHEN

24'-0"
16'-0"

8'-6" 2'-8"

12'-0" 8'-0" 12'-0"
32'-0"

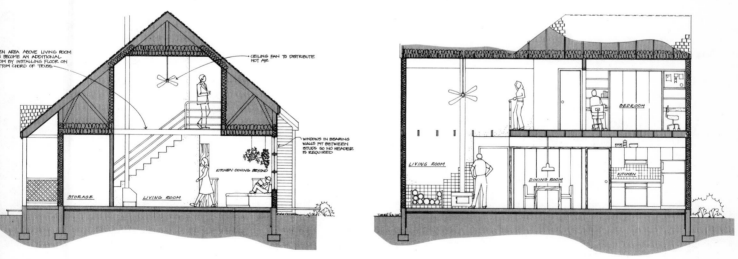

OPEN AREA ABOVE LIVING ROOM CAN BECOME AN ADDITIONAL ROOM BY INSTALLING FLOOR ON BOTTOM CHORD OF TRUSS

CEILING FAN TO DISTRIBUTE HOT AIR

WINDOWS IN BEARING WALLS FIT BETWEEN STUDS SO NO HEADER IS REQUIRED

KITCHEN-DINING BEYOND

STORAGE   LIVING ROOM

LIVING ROOM

DINING ROOM

BEDROOM

KITCHEN

Section AA

Section BB

TYPICAL
LOUVERED WOOD GRILL WITH
ATTIC VENT BEYOND

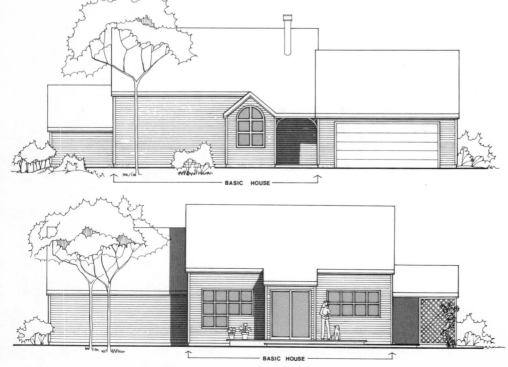

BASIC HOUSE

BASIC HOUSE

1-Roof
235# Asphalt Shingles
15# Felt
½" 48/24 CDX Plywood
10/12 Pitch Engineered
Truss @ 24"O.C.

2-Fascia
1 × 6 Trim
2 × 8 Backer
Continuous Vent

3-Ceiling—8'-0"
Truss Chord @ 24"O.C.
R-50 Blown-in Insulation
6 Mil Vapor Barrier
⅝" Gypsum Board
6" Rigid Urethane
Insulation

4-Truss
Engineered Truss, Pre-
fabricated Bottom Chord
is Structure for Upper
Level Floor. Walls and
Ceiling of Upper Level
are Formed by Truss.

5-Wall
1" Rigid Urethane
Insulation, R-7
R-19 Fiberglass Batt,
Friction Fit
6 Mil Vapor Barrier
⅝" Gypsum Board

6-Floor & Ceiling
¾" T & G Plywood
⅝" Gypsum Board

2 × 8 Bottom Chord of
Truss

7-Ceiling—8'-0"
R-50 Blown-in Insulation
6 Mil Vapor Barrier
⅝" Gypsum Board

8-Wall
Lap (4" Exposure)
Hardboard Siding
1" Rigid Urethane
Insulation R-7
½" CDX Plywood
Sheathing
R-19 Fiberglass Batt,
Friction Fit
6 Mil Vapor Barrier
⅝" Gypsum Board

2 × 6 Studs @ 24"O.C.

9-Floor
4" Slab on Grade with
Exposed Aggregate
Finish
or Quarry Tile
2" Rigid Extruded
Polystyrene Insulation

10-Footing & Foundation
6" × 36" Concrete Wall
with 2 #4's Horizontal
8" × 16" Continuous
Concrete Footing
w/2 #4's
#4 Dowel @ 32"O.C.

11-1" Rigid Extruded
Polystyrene

Wall Section

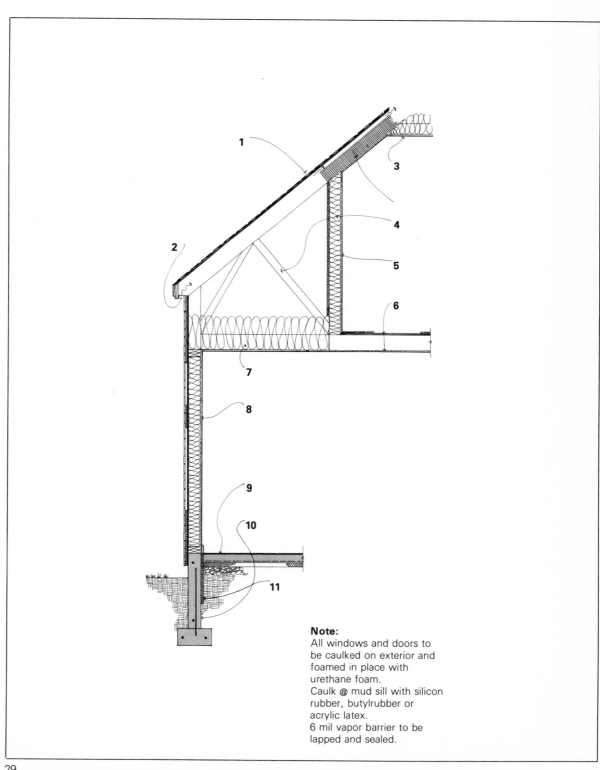

Note:
All windows and doors to
be caulked on exterior and
foamed in place with
urethane foam.
Caulk @ mud sill with silicon
rubber, butylrubber or
acrylic latex.
6 mil vapor barrier to be
lapped and sealed.

Perspective

Good use of the diagonal axis as an organizational device.
Don Metz, judge

A good plan.
Barry Berkus, judge

Russian fireplace with high ceiling hot air intakes down through fireplace mass.
Marc Camens, architect

Camens

Marc Camens

Here's a house built to blunt the sharp thrust of wintery winds in northern New York, to heighten the enjoyment of the beauties of a rural setting. Tucked into a south-sloping site, it offers 996 square feet of spaciousness through use of two floor levels and an open living space linked with a broad deck. The huge mass of the Russian fireplace, the tile and concrete floors, and the masonry walls promise warmth long after the fire's embers have cooled.

It is a home for those who love the outdoors.

When Marc and his wife were discussing the competition, she suggested he design a house for their beautiful woodland acres. He did. When she saw the design, she had the last words:

"Now, let's build it."

They plan to.

By Marc Camens

An Outline
- Earth-sheltered concept in harmony with south-sloping building site.
- Southern exposure has beautiful view of constantly running stream.
- Privacy. The six-acre site adjoins hundreds of acres of pastures, meadows, and forest.
- A wind-sheltered forest cove.
- Natural landscaping. The open forest floor. The house area and play area are grassed.
- Sandy gravel loam soil. Good percolation.
- Russian fireplace with high ceiling hot air intakes down through fireplace mass.
- Mass storage. Tile and concrete floors, and masonry walls.
- Economical removable night insulation of fabric-covered urethane panels.
- Structural bay truss system, long span decking. Ease of construction.

Technical Data
Gross square feet
996
Location
North Bangor, New York
9,500 degree days
Elevation, 700 feet

Materials
Masonry and wood frame walls, heavy timber truss, tongue-and-groove wooden decks, concrete slab with tile and carpet, one-inch insulated glazing, fixed and vent windows, pine siding, gypsum board interior walls with pine decorative walls

Type
Passive solar, earth-sheltered

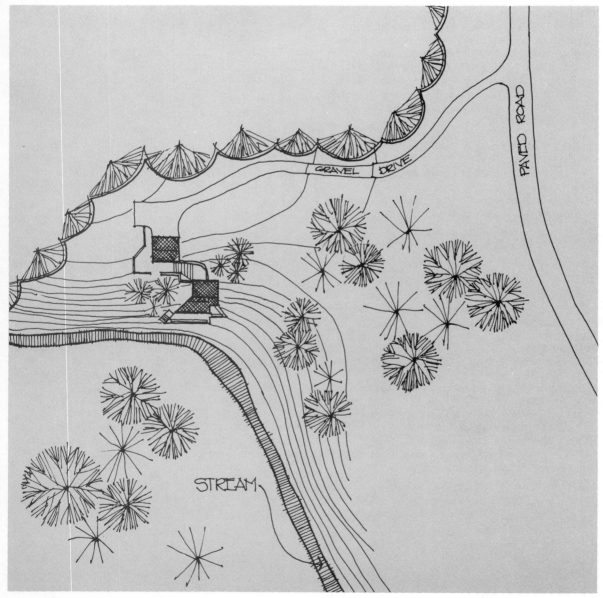

PAVED ROAD

GRAVEL DRIVE

STREAM

Site Plan

Perspective

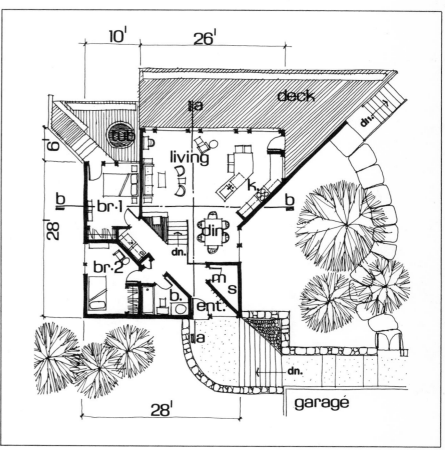

Floor Plan

33

Section AA

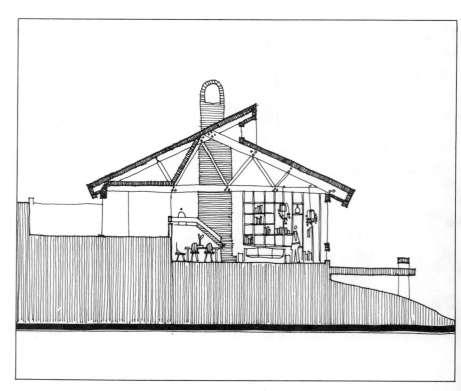

Section BB

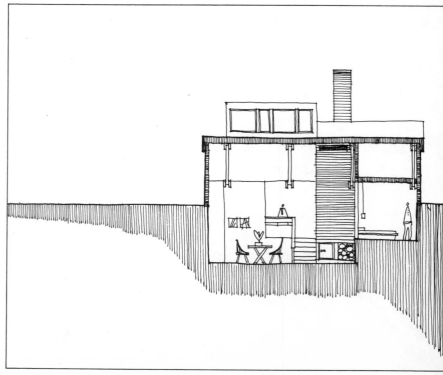

Wall Section

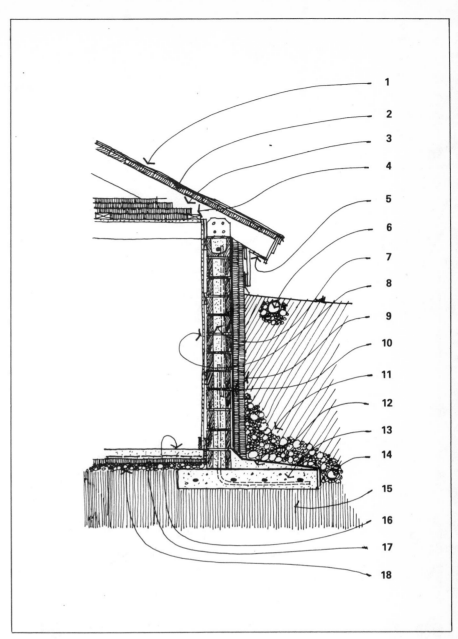

1-Asphalt Shingles Over
   15# Felt
2-2 × 6 T&G Wood Deck
3-Heavy Timber Trusses
4-5″ Urethane Foam-Foil
   Faced
5-Vent Strip Cont.
6-Upper 4″ Perforated
   Drain
7-10″ C.M.U. Reinf. &
   Conc Filled
8-½″ Gyp. Bd on Furring
   Strips

9-4″ Polystyrene Insulation
10-Waterproof Membrane
11-Gravel Fill
12-Footer Drainage Cant
13-Reinforced Cantilever
   Ftg.
14-4″ Perforated Drain &
   Filter
15-Undisturbed Earth
16-4″ Reinf. Conc. Slab
17-1″ Polystyrene Insulation
18-Gravel Fill

Southeast Perspective

Fun . . . but expensive.
John Hix, judge

The cottage elegant, shingle style in a teacup.
Don Metz, judge

Superinsulation gives the typical wall section an R value of 36 . . . Rigid insulating shutters are used on the three biggest south-facing windows while insulating curtains are used over the others.
Robert Coolidge, designer

Coolidge

Robert T. Coolidge

Picture this graceful house in its setting—an array of windows and a broad porch, all looking south toward Long Island Sound.

It's a house that invites relaxation, bids you to take time to taste the beauty of the setting, suggests a life-style of informality and deep enjoyment.

The house was designed for the Connecticut shore, but it would move easily to other sites of beauty, from the coast of Maine to the mountains and shores of the Northwest.

The designer has packed ideas from the centuries into this house. Result: the grace and beauty of yester-years combined with the energy-saving practicalities of today.

By Robert T. Coolidge

The development of this house is based on principles spanning three centuries of tradition in Connecticut houses:

1780s. The plan organization is basically that of the two-over-two center chimney house so common to New England in the 1780s. In this case, however, the simple chimney is replaced by the greater complexity of today's machines. Further, this center dematerial-izes on the first floor to provide an open plan of the living room, kitchen, and dining room for greater spaciousness.

1880s. The stern exterior of the colonial house is replaced by the more generous and flamboyant shingle style so common to the Connecticut shoreline in the 1880s.

1980s. The detailing of this house follows the necessities of the 1980s. Superinsulation gives the walls an R value of 36. Insulating windows with movable insulation helps to cut heat loss through the glass. Rigid insulating shutters are used on the three biggest south-facing windows while insulating curtains are used over the others. Concentrating the windows on the south also helps to increase gains in the winter, while the porch diminishes unwanted gain in the summer.

Technical Data
Project
Compact House on Long Island Sound
Gross square feet
975

Location
Connecticut shoreline
5,100-5,800 degree days
Materials
Wood frame, CMU foundation, cedar shingles
Type
Superinsulated

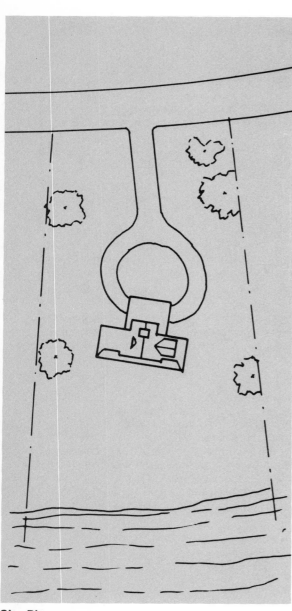

Site Plan

Perspective

Second Floor Plan

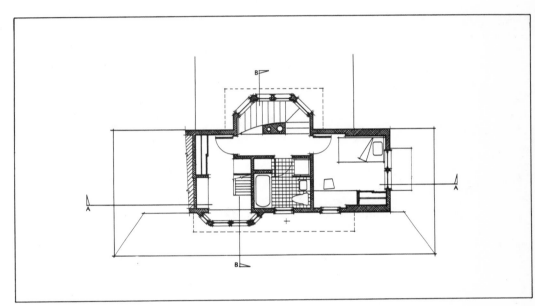

First Floor Plan

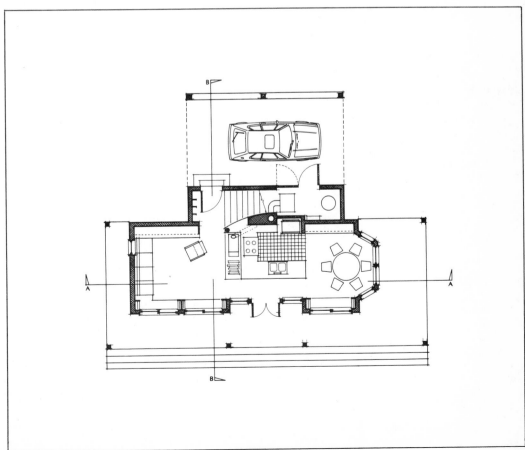

39

Section AA

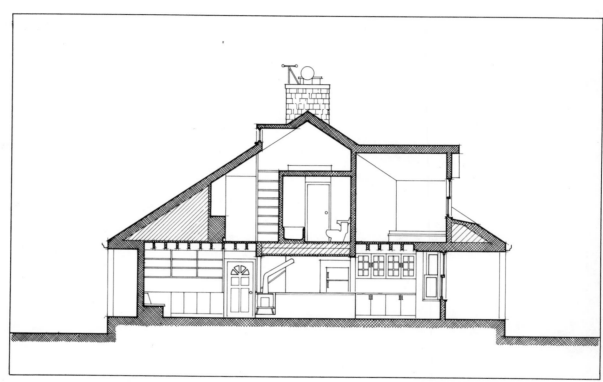

Section BB

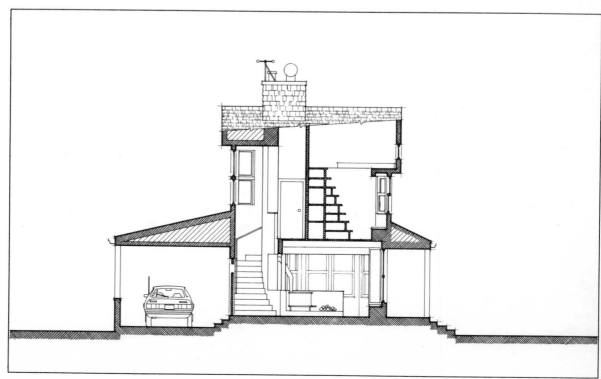

Master Bedroom

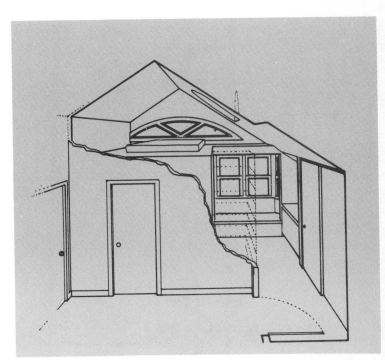

Stair and Kitchen

41

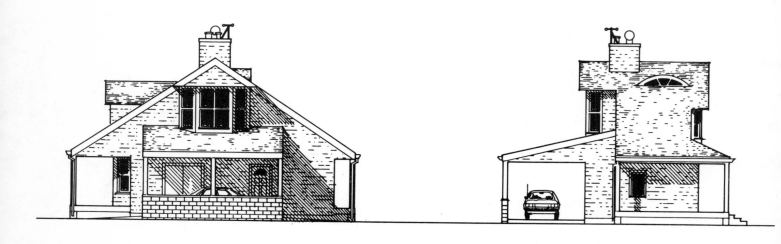

/all Section

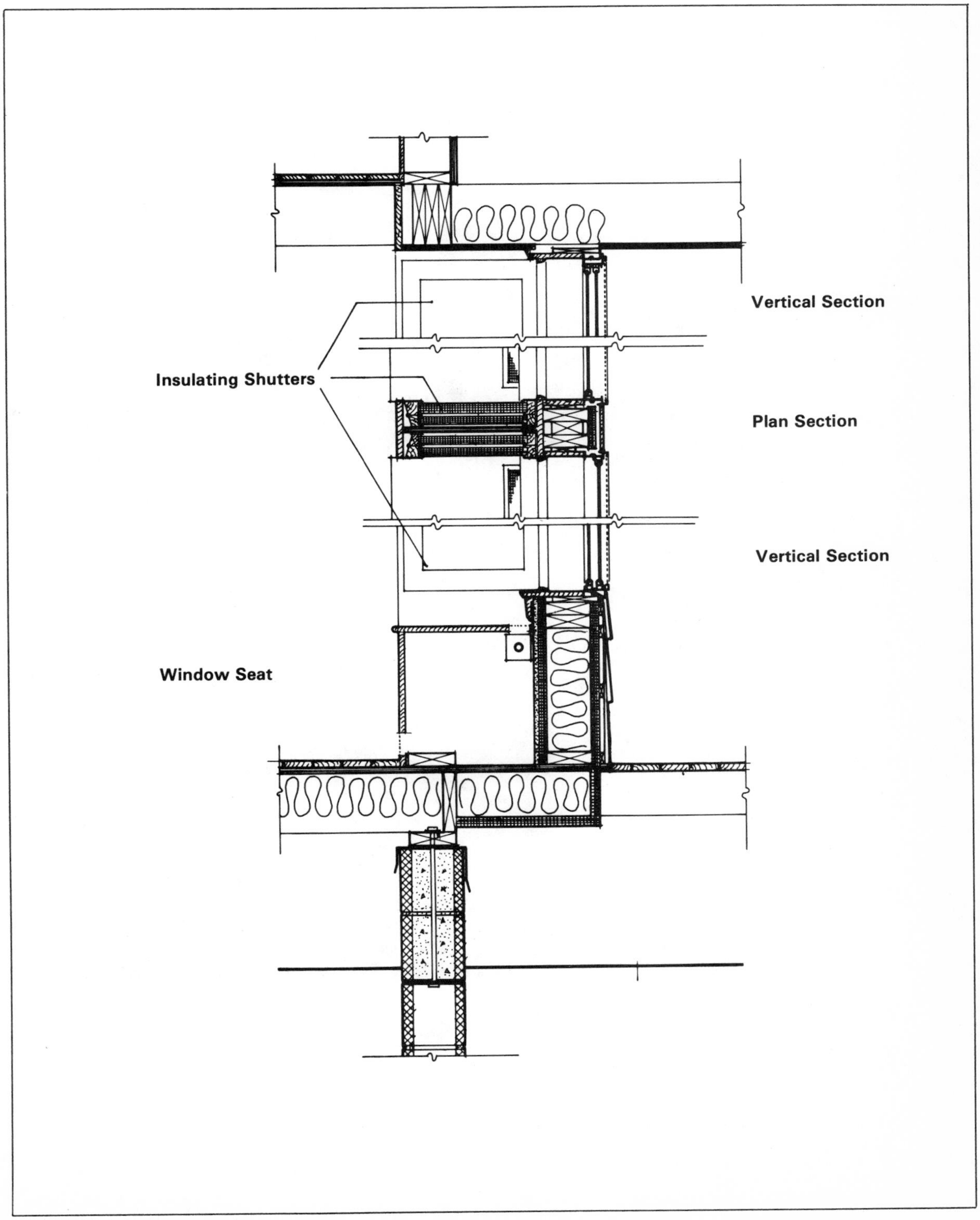

Vertical Section
Insulating Shutters
Plan Section
Vertical Section
Window Seat

Perspective

A good plan for the Southeast climate and all-season comfort.
Don Watson, judge

A very open design.
Ralph Johnson, judge

It is a house that says small but smart and does so with confidence.
Dail Dixon, architect

44

Dixon

ail Dixon

This, one judge concluded, is a home that works.

Its passive solar design will contribute heat during the chill of winter; when the weather turns warm, the venting cupola will pull in fresh air and discharge the warm air from the house. The bedroom ell is set apart from the living area, and this separateness is accented by a step leading down to the two bedrooms and bath.

Those who live in this house will grow to love its many features. The dining area, so delightful in the morning, with its east-facing windows. The strength, mass, and practicality of the "hearth," giving back the heat from the wood stove it spans long after the fire is out. The spaciousness accented by the high ceilings and the skylight. The foyer and storage space, so often slighted in the compact house.

By Dail Dixon

The design assumes a client with reordered priorities, a client interested in quality rather than quantity for his housing dollar. The results are quality space, details, and materials; passive heating and cooling; and style. It is a house that says small but smart and does so with confidence.

The central space focuses on the "hearth," a brick column which vents the wood stove, supports a sheltering hip roof and its venting cupola, and provides an organizing element for the smaller spaces within the family area. The space opens up to the southeast for a distant horizon view and to the sun.

The bedroom ell clusters around the southwest corner, sheltering the family space from the prevailing breeze. A step down into this area heightens the sense of separation from the public spaces.

On the north and east of the family space are projections for the mechanical/laundry room and a banquette seating bay for both eating and socializing in the kitchen/dining area. A table in this area doubles for workspace and dining. There is a shelving wall on the west of the central space which could accommodate a small desk should that be desirable. The "living room" space is highlighted by a skylight which focuses on the brick "hearth" and by its proximity to the view.

Technical Data
Project
Compact House
Gross square feet
950
Location
Chatham County, North Carolina
3,514 degree days
Elevation, 562 feet

Materials
Wood, block foundation, aluminum windows, cedar siding, asphalt shingles
Type
Passive solar

45

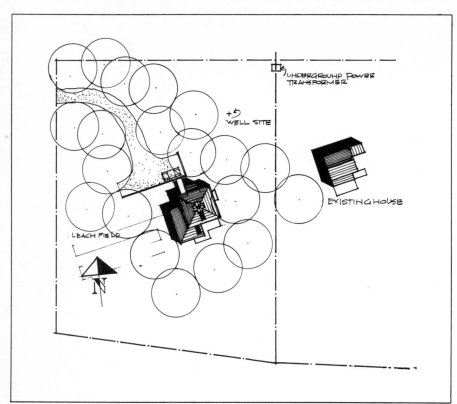

Site Plan

The house is capable of providing approximately 45 percent of its heating needs with 266 square feet of south glazing coupled with water tubes, brick floors, and the brick column for thermal mass. In the summer all south-facing glazing is shaded by building overhangs or acrylic awnings. The venting cupola creates a thermal chimney for ventilation. For back-up heating there is an electric heat pump which would be installed with a high return to enable its fan system to function for air circulation. There are also air tubes mounted on the brick column and a fan system in the bedroom space which help to circulate solar and wood stove heat.

A small house with an eye to quality and the future.

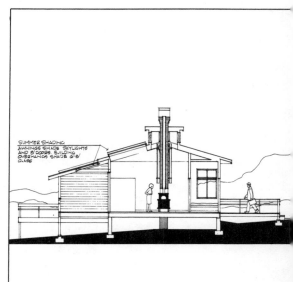

Section AA

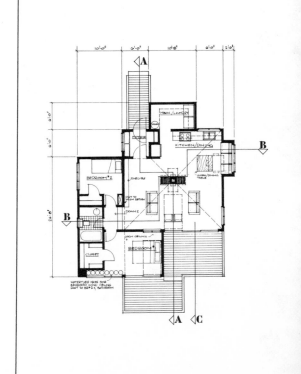

Floor Plan

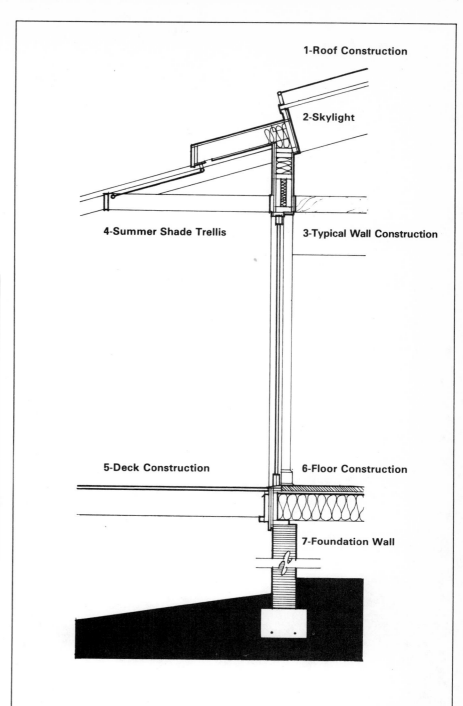

1-Roof Construction

2-Skylight

4-Summer Shade Trellis

3-Typical Wall Construction

5-Deck Construction

6-Floor Construction

7-Foundation Wall

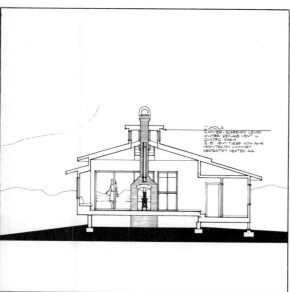

CUPOLA
SUMMER-SCREENED VENTS
WINTER-EXPLAIN VENT W
GLAZED EACH
2-8' VENT TUBES WITH FANS
MOUNTED ON CHIMNEY
DESTRATIFY HEATED AIR

Section BB

Wall Section

1-Roof Construction
235# Asp. Fiberglass
Shingles
½" Plywood
R—30 Batts (Sloped Ceil.)
R38 Flat Ceil.
2-Skylight
Acrylic Shade Awning
(Manual Installation on
Pipe Frame)
Double Glazed Fiberglass
Skylight
3-Typical Wall Construction
2 × 6 Studs 24"O.C.
¾" Insulating Sheathing

+ R—19 Batts
4 Mil Poly Vapor Barrier
½" Sheetrock
1 × 6 Picture Mold at 8'
Exterior
1 × 8 Stained "German"
Cedar Siding to 8'-1 × 6
Painted Trim Board—
Painted Overlay Plywood
Above
4-Summer Shade Trellis
2 × 6 Frame w/¾" I.D.
Gal. Pipe
Acrylic Shade

5-Deck Construction
1 × 6 Pressure Treated
Pine
on 2 × 10 Joists
6-Floor Construction
1⅝" Brick in Family Space
Carpet in Bedrooms
Tile in Bathroom
2 × 10 Joists 16"O.C.
R—30 Batts
6 Mil Poly on Earth
7-Foundation Wall
8" Block w/Stucco
16 × 10" Conc. Footing

Perspective

This is an intriguing use of
berm and tepee, solids ver-
sus light. Although the plan
is very formal, the lack of
partitions dictates an in-
formal lifestyle.
Don Metz, judge

The interior spaces are designed as a series of small
spaces burrowing and com-
bining to create a living platform.
Richard Dunham, designer

Dunham

Richard Dunham

The interior is designed as a series of small spaces burrowing and combining to create a living platform. Under the platform is a thermo plenum crawl space that consists of PVC pipe filled with water between the floor joists. The HVAC system forces hot/cold air down into the plenum, creating a thermo sink with three return air ducts. One is at eighteen feet for use in the winter only. The other two are at nine feet above floor level, and are for summer use.

Prairie One has the option of additional studio/ bedroom space above the core between the two roof trusses.

The use of huge precast concrete pipes for entrances suggests the unusual features to be found in this house.

By Richard Dunham

The concept of Prairie One is a passive thermo sink plenum/superinsulated solar syphon from which hot air rises to the top. It is vented by an operable skylight in conjunction with awning windows in the passive solar wall to maintain positive ventilation. The awning windows are approximately three times larger in surface area than the skylight at the top solar syphon.

The air lock entries are on the east and west walls. They are made of eight-foot-square, precast concrete storm sewer pipes with sliding glass doors at either end.

Prairie One assumes a very active owner who is a "do-it-yourself" type person. The hermatic environment of Prairie One with its ivy-covered earth berm on three sides of the living space affords the use of earth and nature to enclose the house. The earth berm is constructed of loose rubble and compact fill so as to maintain its shape and insulation integrity. The passive solar wall is the open glazed side which faces the south with a view of an open field. Deciduous trees line the south side, shading the passive solar wall during the summer and allowing heat gain during the winter.

Technical Data
Project
Prairie One
Gross square feet
900
Location
Stillwater, Oklahoma
4,754 degree days.
Elevation, 900 feet

Materials
Poured-in-place concrete piers, wood framing, corrugated metal roof
Type
Passive plenum/solar syphon with ivy-covered earth berm, superinsulated walls

Site Plan

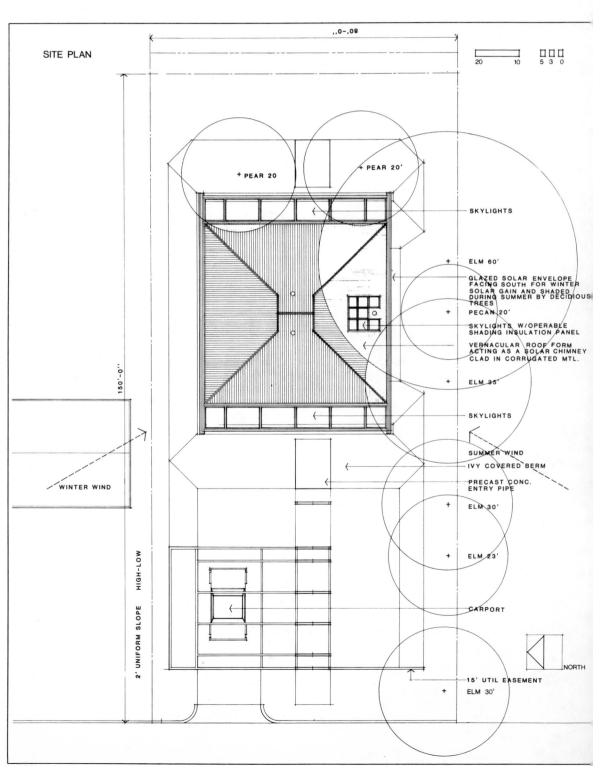

SITE PLAN

80'-0"

20   10   5 3 0

+ PEAR 20

+ PEAR 20'

SKYLIGHTS

ELM 60'

GLAZED SOLAR ENVELOPE
FACING SOUTH FOR WINTER
SOLAR GAIN AND SHADED
DURING SUMMER BY DECIDIOUS
TREES

PECAN 20'

SKYLIGHTS W/OPERABLE
SHADING INSULATION PANEL

VERNACULAR ROOF FORM
ACTING AS A SOLAR CHIMNEY
CLAD IN CORRUGATED MTL.

ELM 35'

SKYLIGHTS

SUMMER WIND

IVY COVERED BERM

PRECAST CONC.
ENTRY PIPE

ELM 30'

ELM 23'

CARPORT

15' UTIL EASEMENT

ELM 30'

NORTH

150'-0"

WINTER WIND

2' UNIFORM SLOPE   HIGH-LOW

Floor Plan

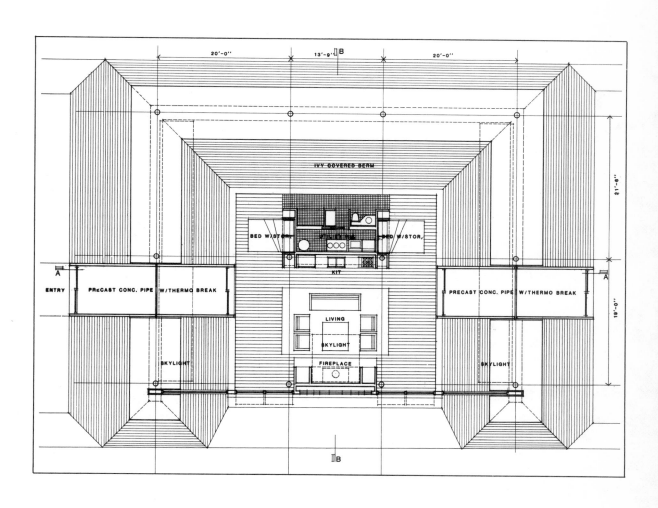

Section AA

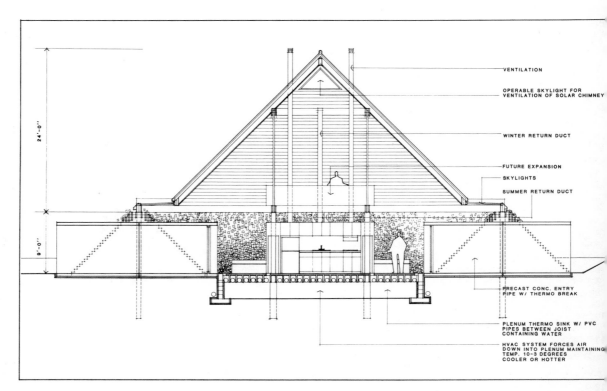

VENTILATION

OPERABLE SKYLIGHT FOR
VENTILATION OF SOLAR CHIMNEY

WINTER RETURN DUCT

FUTURE EXPANSION

SKYLIGHTS

SUMMER RETURN DUCT

PRECAST CONC. ENTRY
PIPE W/ THERMO BREAK

PLENUM THERMO SINK W/ PVC
PIPES BETWEEN JOIST
CONTAINING WATER

HVAC SYSTEM FORCES AIR
DOWN INTO PLENUM MAINTAINING
TEMP. 10-3 DEGREES
COOLER OR HOTTER

24'-0"

9'-0"

Section BB

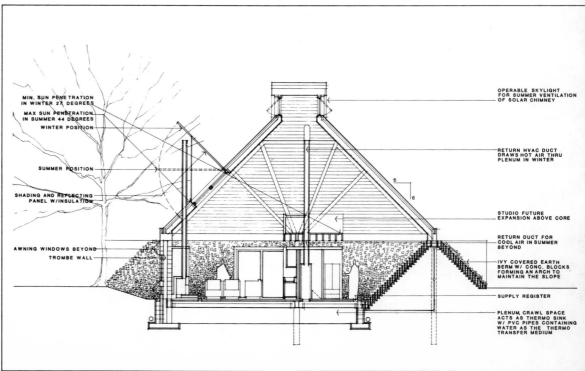

MIN. SUN PENETRATION
IN WINTER 27 DEGREES

MAX SUN PENETRATION
IN SUMMER 44 DEGREES

WINTER POSITION

SUMMER POSITION

SHADING AND REFLECTING
PANEL W/INSULATION

AWNING WINDOWS BEYOND

TROMBE WALL

OPERABLE SKYLIGHT
FOR SUMMER VENTILATION
OF SOLAR CHIMNEY

RETURN HVAC DUCT
DRAWS HOT AIR THRU
PLENUM IN WINTER

STUDIO FUTURE
EXPANSION ABOVE CORE

RETURN DUCT FOR
COOL AIR IN SUMMER
BEYOND

IVY COVERED EARTH
BERM W/ CONC. BLOCKS
FORMING AN ARCH TO
MAINTAIN THE SLOPE

SUPPLY REGISTER

PLENUM CRAWL SPACE
ACTS AS THERMO SINK
W/ PVC PIPES CONTAINING
WATER AS THE THERMO
TRANSFER MEDIUM

1-Built-Up Truss 2 × 4
2-Corrugated Mtl. Cladding
3-3″ Rigid Insulation Roof Decking R6 w/Roofing Felt
4-6″ Batten Insulation R19
5-2 × 8 Ceiling Rafters 16″O.C.
6-Vapor Barrier
7-1 × 8 T&G Fin. Ceiling
8-Skylight
9-Mtl. Rake Closure
10-2-2 × 12 Built Up w/Rigid Insulation
11-45 Degree Slope Maintained By 8″ Sq. Conc. Blocks Forming an Arch w/Keystone
12-Precast Conc. Storm Pipe w/Thermo Break
13-Compact Fill Earth Berm
14-Supply Register
15-Chain Link Fence w/Vapor Barrier and Rigid Insulation
16-Vapor Barrier
17-Conc. Footing w/Conc. Blk. Stem Wall Filled w/Vermiculite
18-Super Insulated Thermo Plenum
19-8″ Concrete Pip. Pier
20-Drainage Pipe
21-8″ Dia. PVC Pipe w/Water Capped on Ends, Wire Mesh Supports PVC Thermo Sink
22-Vapor Barrier
23-2 × 12 Floor Joist 12″O.C.
24-1 × 8 T&G Floor w/¾″ Ply Wd Subfloor
25-12″ Conc. Pip. Pier

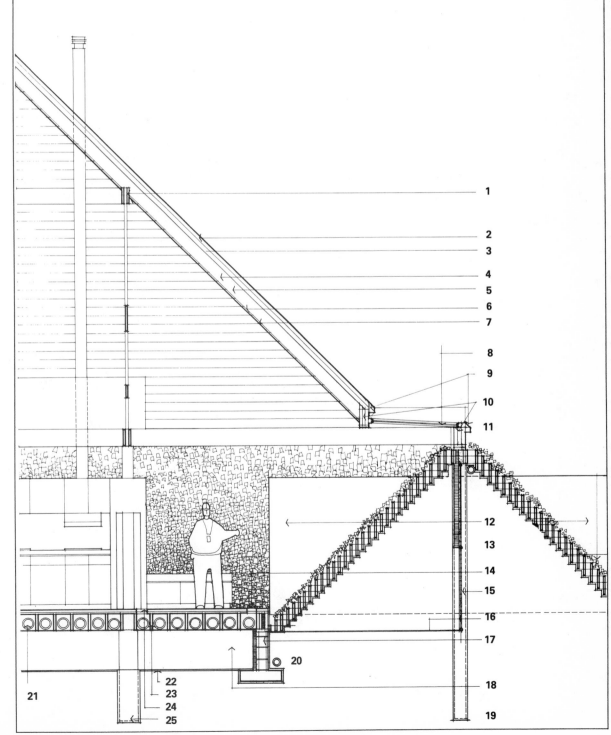

53

Perspective

This is a very straightforward plan, with a variety of space size, volume, and indoor-outdoor choices. Excellent.
Don Watson, judge

There's a great deal of flexibility in the living space.
Bob Giddings, architect

Giddings

Bob Giddings

Here's a design that promises energy efficiency and spaciousness.

For energy efficiency — a wood stove, passive solar heat, a heat pump, heavy insulation, thermal mass, skylights with insulating shutters and awnings, transoms for ventilation, a porch that can be walled in.

For spaciousness — a living/family-activity area (one-third of the house's floor space) plus an adjoining open kitchen, a cathedral ceiling over the living area, a screened porch and deck.

Here's a simple design that works.

By Bob Giddings

The site is in a rural neighborhood on a 1½-acre lot which slopes gently away from the road to a creek on the south side and is heavily wooded with deciduous trees. Temperatures in the immediate area are generally 5°-10° cooler than the nearest reporting station, and the prevailing winds are from the northwest.

The house is of direct gain passive solar design with a covered or screened porch which can be converted into a solarium in the winter by attaching clear awning material or glass storm panels. An insulating shutter for the skylights over the living room pivots at the ridge to store against the opposite ceiling when open.

Brick floors are used in conjunction with clear water tubes in the cabinets behind the couches for thermal mass.

Wall construction is 2 × 6s with R-19 insulation; the floors and ceilings have R-30-38 insulation.

In the summer, awnings are placed over the skylights to prevent overheating, operable windows in the gable ends over the living room offer natural ventilation, and a whole-house attic fan is planned. Transoms are used over the bedroom doors to maintain privacy while providing ventilation. Supplemental heat comes from a centrally located wood stove. The projected heating costs are based on an electric air-to-air heat pump.

There's a great deal of flexibility in the living space: the kitchen table can be rotated to seat six, and two additional sleeping areas can be provided by rotating the two L-shaped couches face-to-face to create two full-sized beds.

This house was designed for an exciting and spacious-feeling living environment for people desiring the smaller house.

Technical Data
Project
Compact House DW-II
Gross square feet
1,000
Location
Chapel Hill, North Carolina
3,514 degree days
Elevation, 527 feet

Materials
Wood, Brick, Sheetrock
Type
Passive solar

Site Plan

Labels within the figure: 10% Slope · VIEW · PREVAILING WIND

Floor Plan

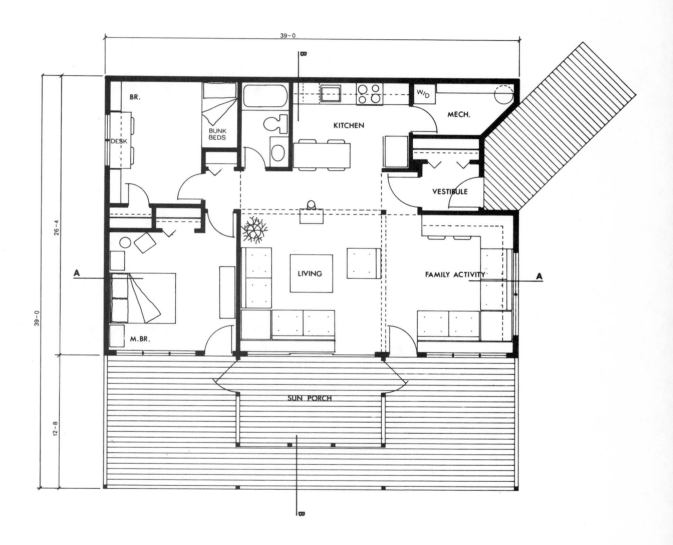

Section AA

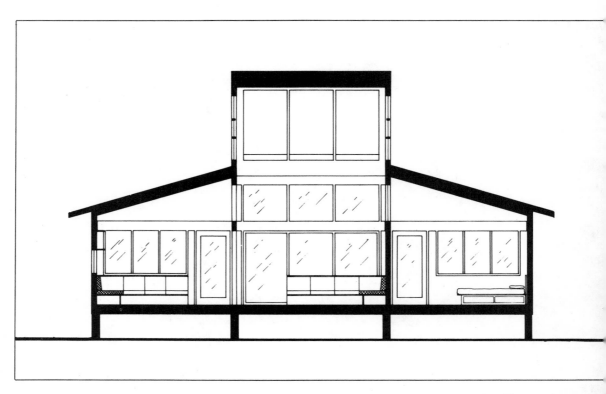

Section BB

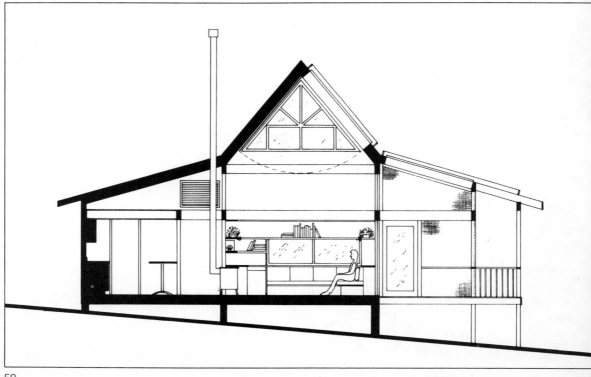

Wall Section

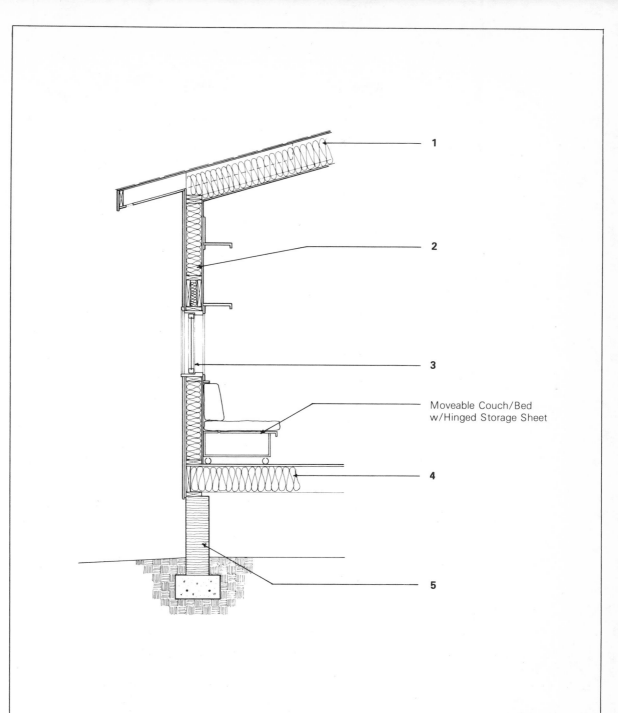

1

2

3

Moveable Couch/Bed
w/Hinged Storage Sheet

4

5

1-Roof Construction
240 # Asphalt Shingles on
15 # Bldg. Felt on ½"
Plywood w/H-Clips on
Roof Trusses or 2 × 12's
@ 24" O.C. w/R-30 Batt
Insul. Over 4 Mil Vapor
Barrier

**2-Exterior Wall
Construction**
Siding (Owner's Choice)
on ½" Foil Faced Foam
Sheathing on 2 × 6 Studs
@ 24" O.C. w/Let in
Diagonal Bracing & R-19
Batt Insulation w/½"
Drywall Over 4 Mil Vapor
Barrier

**3-Windows & Sliding
Glass Doors**
Windows are Wood
Casement, Awnings &
Fixed w/Thermopane
Glass Sliding Glass Doors
are Bronze Finish
Aluminum w/Thermal
Break & Thermopane

4-Floor Construction
Finish Floor (Owner's
Choice) on ¼" T&G
Plywood on 2 × 10's @
16" O.C. w/R-30 Batt
Insul. w/4 Mil Vapor
Barrier on Ground
5-Foundation Construction
3" Scored Conc. Block on
Continuous Concrete
Footing w/Continuous
Steel Reinforcing

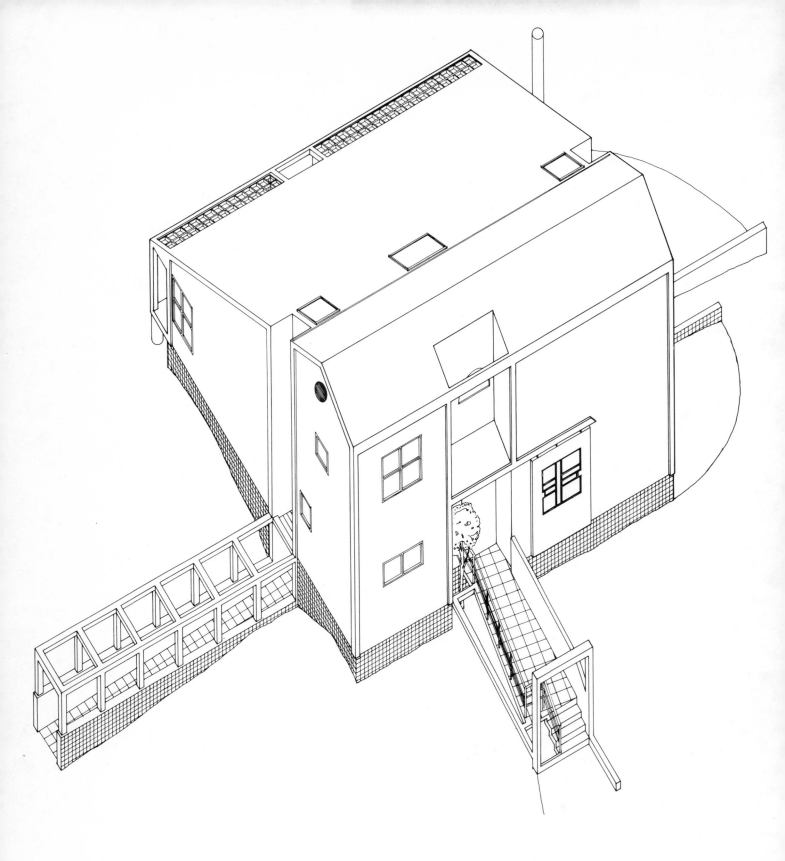

Axonometric

Lots of action here. An economical shell with a variety of post-modernist devices mixed in for spice. Don Metz, judge

This skylight spine acts as a passive collector with the stratified warm air recirculated by a simple fan system. . . . Adam Gross, architect

Gross

dam Gross

The intermediate zone between these two spaces contains the stairs and hallway, and it is skylit, reinforcing the split between the two zones. This skylit spine acts as a passive collector with the stratified warm air recirculated by a simple fan system, to be reused throughout the house.

The image of the house is not trying to be "postmodern." Rather, it is an attempt to inject a geometric ordering device, combined with simple solar principles, into a typology of regional architecture. The result is the creation of highly organized, compact service/private areas, juxtaposed with an airy, open living/public space.

There's a satisfying spaciousness about this house. The open stairway, two-story living area, and the skylight cleverly beaming light down to the first floor all contribute to this.

By Adam Gross

The site is seven acres of heavily wooded land in northern Massachusetts. The house was sited on a small knoll to take maximum advantage of the views and southern orientation.

The house takes its form from the traditional saltbox shape with the major roof sloping to the south.

This space is then separated into private and public zones, with the private (bedroom, bathrooms, and kitchen) being cut away and articulated, leaving a simple, gabled volume.

This "little house" is the solid portion with small windows to the north. The public zone (living/dining room) is the remainder of the saltbox with floor-to-ceiling, south-facing glass and a sloping, two-story shed roof.

Technical Data
Project
Feeley Residence
Gross square feet
900
Location
Boxford, Massachusetts
6,000 degree days
Elevation, 200 feet

Materials
Poured concrete foundation walls, 2 x 6 stud walls with five-inch batt insulation and two-inch rigid insulation, Andersen Permashield windows, 2 x 7 roof rafters with 9½-inch batt insulation

Type
Passive solar heating with recirculated, stratified hot-air combined with superinsulation

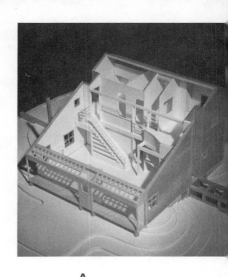

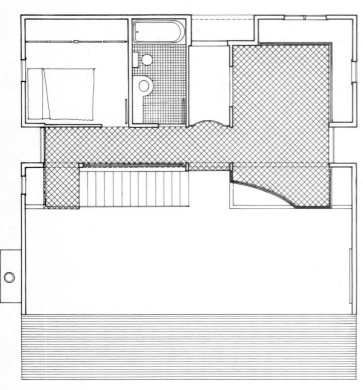

Upper Level Plan

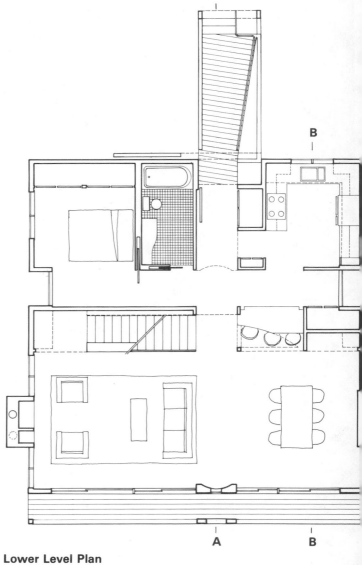

A

B

A   B

Lower Level Plan

63

Site Plan

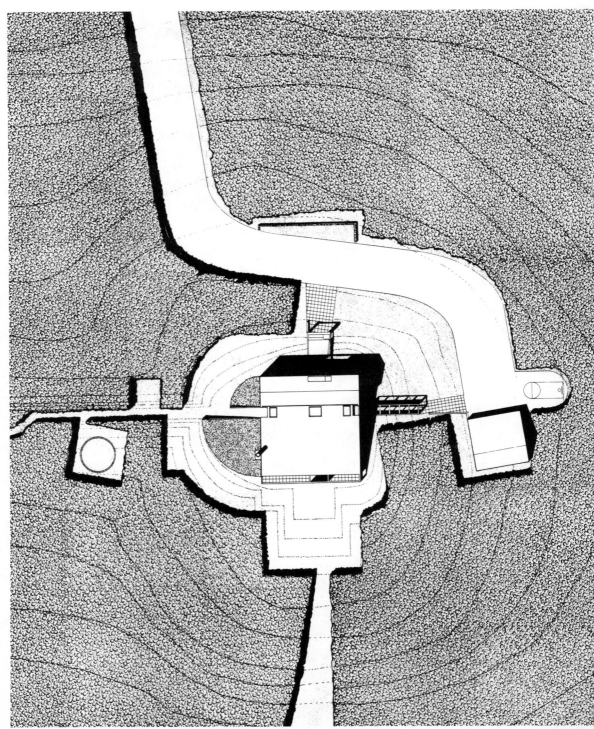

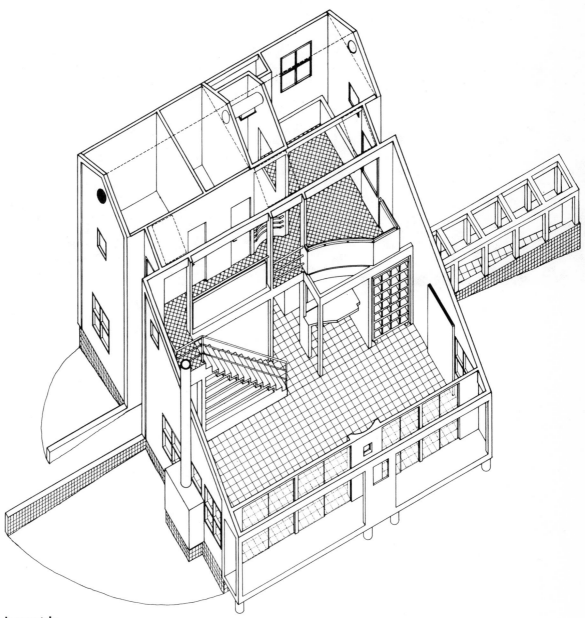

Isometric

Wall Section

1-Asphalt Shingles
2-¾" Plywood
3-2 × 10 Rafter
4-9" Batt Insulation
  R Value = R40
5-Copper Gutter
6-Crown Molding
7-Continuous Vent Strip
8-½" Gyp. Board
9-¾" Hardwood Flooring
10-¾" Plywood Subfloor
11-6" Painted Wood
  Baseboard
12-Andersen Permashield
  Window
13-½" Ext. T&G Clear Pine
  Siding
14-1½" Rigid Insulation

15-½" Plywood Sheathing
16-5" Batt Insulation
17-2" × 6" Wood Studs @
  16" O.C.
18-Vapor Barrier
  R Value = R20
19-9" Batt Insulation
20-¾" Furring Strips
21-½" Gyp. Board
22-Moisture/Vapor Barrier
23-2" Rigid Insulation
24-¾" Furring Strips
25-10" Thick Concrete
26-Foundation Wall
27-½" Expansion Joint
28-4" Concrete Slab
29-Moisture/Vapor Barrier

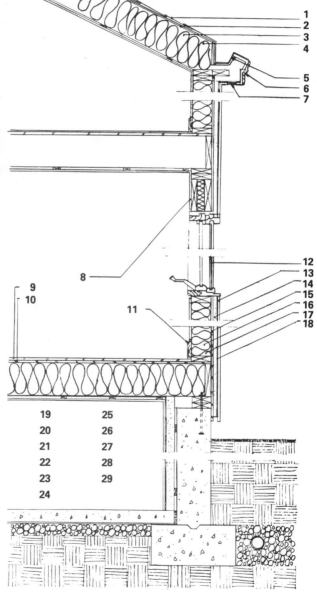

1
2
3
4
5
6
7
8
9
10
11
12
13
14
15
16
17
18

19   25
20   26
21   27
22   28
23   29
24

Site Plan

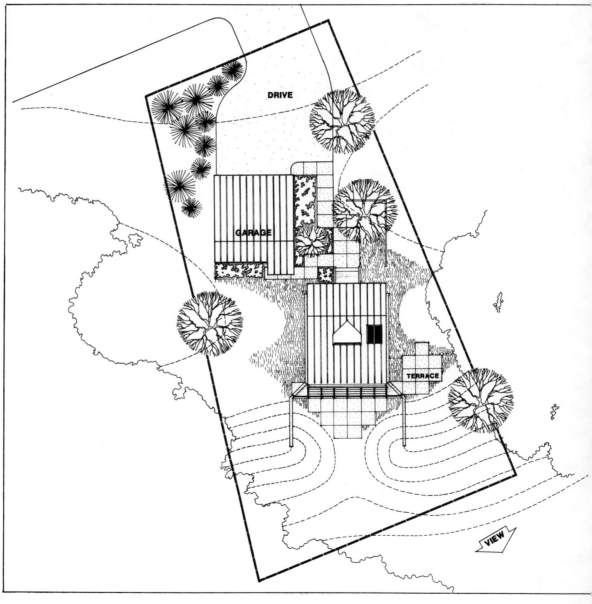

A handsome, nostalgic form with a compact circulation pattern and innovative use of the traditional central chimney.
Don Metz, judge

This compact design has been developed from the Connecticut saltbox of colonial times. . . .
Thomas M. Haskell, architect

Haskell

Thomas M. Haskell

This house is an excellent example of fitting an old design to today's needs, with its emphasis on conservation of energy.

The furnace shown on the ground level floor plan can be vented up through the coat closet and the staircase.

The loft is an added bonus for reading, writing, or an extra sleeping bag over the holidays. The "solar chimney" acts as a thermal storage mass against solar gain and tempers incoming make-up air for wood stove combustion.

By Thomas M. Haskell

The building site is part of a wooded acreage being subdivided for single-family homes. The 7,500-square-foot lot is situated in a clearing at the top of a knoll with southeast views of Long Island Sound. Four large maples are to remain. The south-facing slope is ideal for passive solar techniques. Summer breezes blow off the water while winter storms buffet the shore from south and west. Underlying soil is a stable, gravelly clay with good bearing characteristics.

This compact design has been developed from the Connecticut saltbox of colonial times, inverted to place bedrooms below the main living space. The building volume is nearly square to reduce surface area. Interior spaces are continuous and an entry lock is provided.

A metal roof reflects uncontrolled radiation; windows and translucent panels admit and diffuse controlled sunlight. Night insulation (R-9) is provided by sliding and hinged panels.

The principle energy feature is a concrete masonry solar chimney which concentrates storage mass and admits daylight in the center of the house. Additional mass is provided in a thickened ground floor slab. In summer the air is vented to promote natural cooling. Collectors for a solar water heater are mounted on the roof adjacent to the chimney.

Solar techniques provide 92 percent of the heating needs of this home. A wood stove located in the central chimney can easily supply the balance. A furnace provides back-up heat and ventilation.

Technical Data
Project
Compact House
Gross square feet
962
Location
Branford, Connecticut

Materials
Cast-in-place foundation wall, slab on grade, wood framing, gypsum board, double-glazed door and window units, translucent insulated glazing panels, batt insulation (walls R-20, roof, R-40) hardwood flooring, standing seam metal roof (6/12 pitch)

Type
Hybrid passive solar

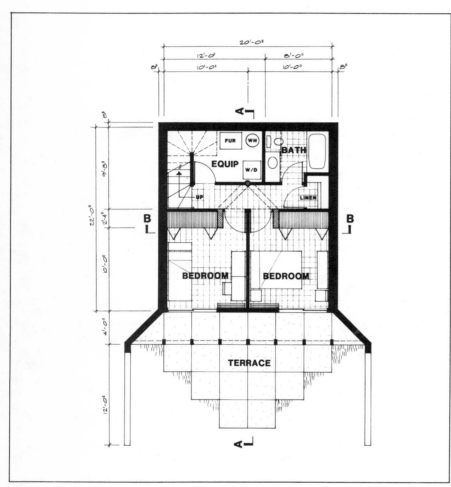

Ground Floor Plan

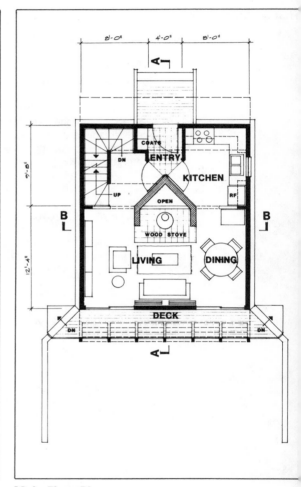

Main Floor Plan

70

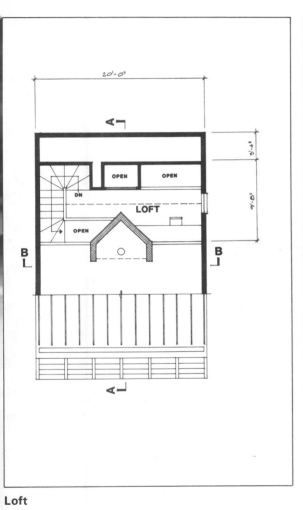

Loft

Perspective

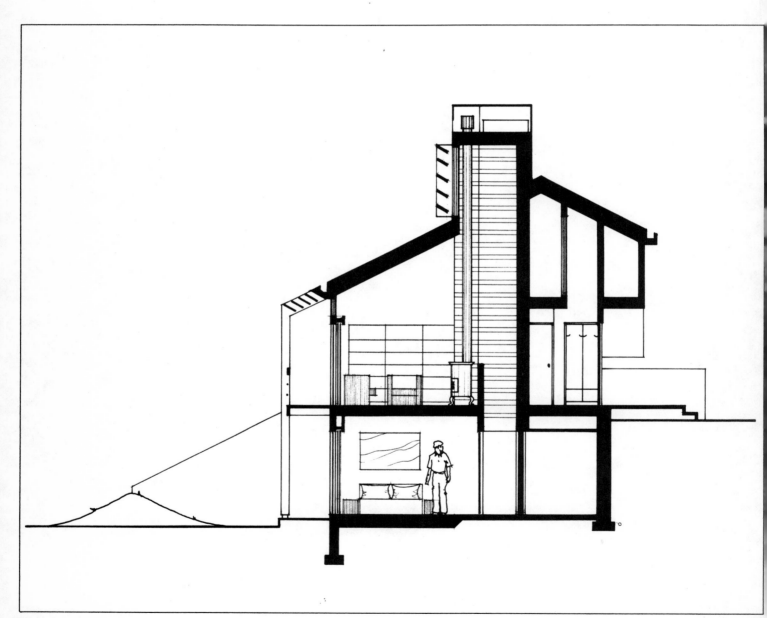

Section AA

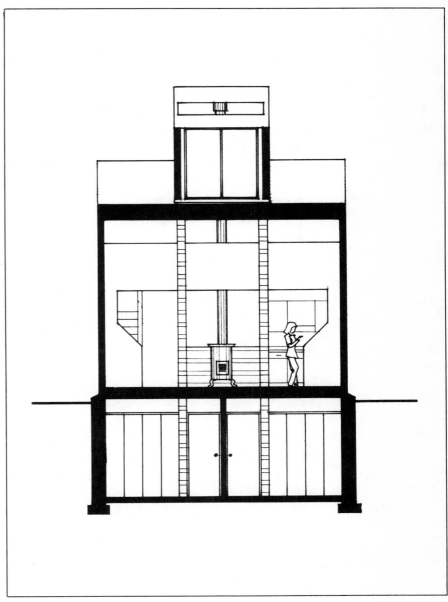

Section BB

South Wall

1-Wood Louvers
2-Wood Sliding Doors
3-Sliding Translucent
   Insulating Panels
4-Hand Rail
5-Light Cove

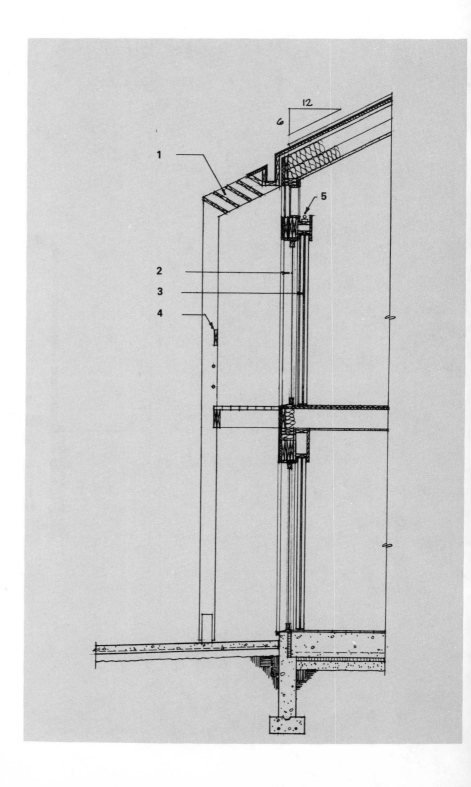

North Wall

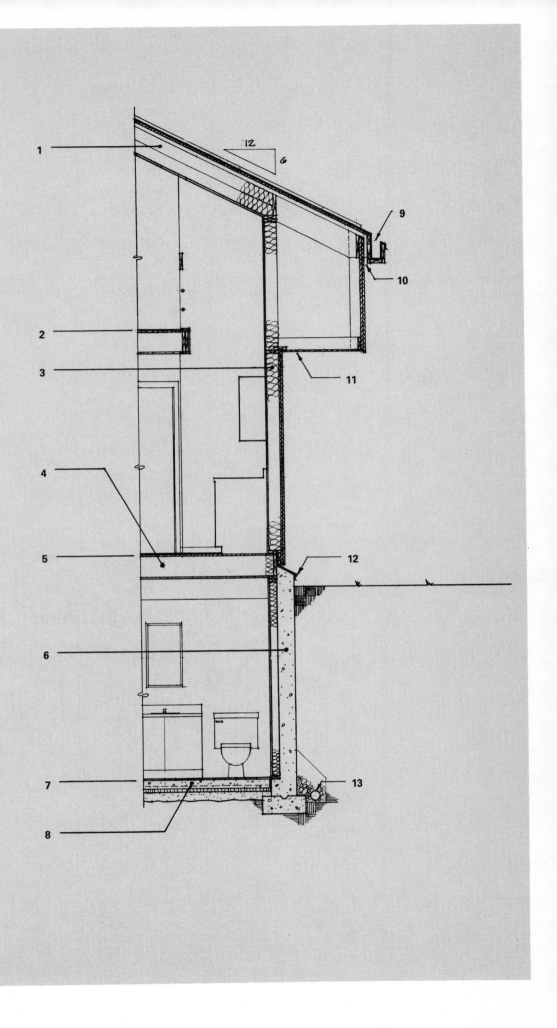

1-Roof
Standing Seam Metal
Roof
⅝″ Plywood
Underlayment
2 × 12 Rafter w/2 × 2
Nailer, 24″ O.C.
12″ Batt Insulation
Vapor Barrier
⅝″ Gypsum Bd.
2-Loft
3-Wall
⅝″ Gypsum Bd.
Vapor Barrier
2 × 6 Studs, 16″ O.C.
Batt Insulation
⅝″ Insul. Sheathing
Horizontal Cedar Siding
4-Floor
Hardwood Flr.
¾″ Plywd. Subfloor
2 × 10 Joists, 16″ O.C.
⅝″ Gypsum Bd.
5-Main Floor
6-Wall
⅝″ Gypsum Bd.
Vapor Barrier
3½″ Studs, 16″ O.C.
Batt Insulation
60 Mil Waterproofing
8″ Conc. Foundation
Wall
7-Ground Floor
8-Floor
Quarry Tile
4″ Concrete Slab
Vapor Barrier
1½″ Rigid Insulation
4″ Sand Cushion
9-Metal Gutter
in Wood Frame
10-Contin. Vent
11-Plywood Soffit
12-Metal Cap Flashing
13-Footing Drain

View from Southwest

Here we see an energetic neo-classicist solution full of function and fun.
Don Metz, judge

The half-level entrance to the house allows a descending approach into the living spaces that is combined with two-story space to give the sense of expanding volume.
J. Whitney Huber, designer

Huber

J. Whitney Huber
The designer of this house was determined that compact would not mean confined. He succeeded.

Note the two-story section of the living room, the openness of the living, dining, and kitchen areas, the balcony of the master bedroom, all contributing to a sense of spaciousness.

By J. Whitney Huber

Hill Hut's goal is to provide comfortable, energy-efficient shelter in a small package without the feeling of confinement. The design uses the elements of surprise, contrast, and view to create a variety of spaces that feel larger than they actually are.

Hill Hut is a passive solar house which presents a protected face to the north and an open one to the south. The house is set into the site to reduce its northern exposure. A half-level entrance to the house, on the north side, allows a descending approach to the living spaces that is combined with two-story space to give the sense of expanding volume both upward and outward to the south. The shell of the house is well insulated to contain heat gained from the winter sun. Solar heat can be stored in the tile-covered concrete floor slab on the lower level and in the large volume of air within the house. A wood or

coal stove can be used to supplement the heating requirements. Summertime cooling is achieved with ample windows arranged to create breezes through all rooms.

The body of Hill Hut, twenty-four feet square in plan, is enhanced by a front porch (which, when fitted with glass panels as shown here, provides a protected winter entrance), a stone terrace off the living areas, and a balcony from the master bedroom. These ancillary elements contribute to the sense of larger space.

Hill Hut can be easily adapted to a variety of site terrains, including those that are flat. Construction costs are reduced by eliminating the usual basement or crawlspace beneath the first floor. The relatively shallow excavation required for this house and the elimination of wood floor framing for the lower level save labor and materials. The selection of finish materials will influence not only the construction costs, but also the personality of the house.

Technical Data
Project
Hill Hut
Gross square feet
997
Location
Essex, Connecticut
Former hillside pasture
5,900 degree days
Elevation, 275 feet

Materials
2 × 6 wood balloon frame construction on concrete foundation, stucco wall system, wood windows and doors, cedar shingle roof, tile and wood floors, gypsum board walls and ceilings
Type
Passive solar with electric or oil back-up

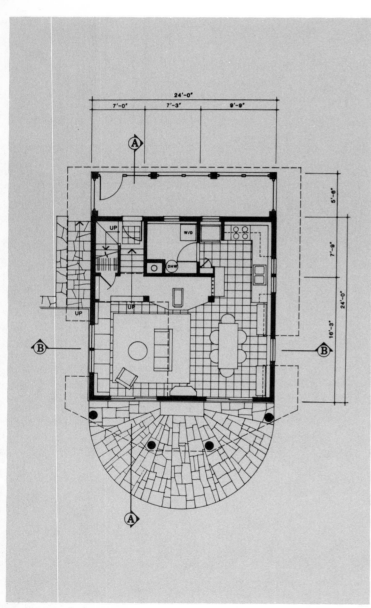

Lower Level Plan

Upper Level Plan

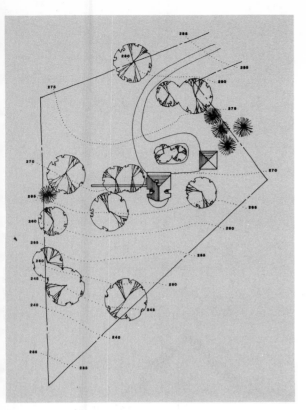

Site Plan

Wall Section

1-⅝" GWB
2-6 Mil VB
3-6" Batt (R19)
4-2 × 6 @ 24" O.C.
5-½" × 2½" Wd. Base
6-½" Cpt. Underlayment
7-¾" Plywd.
8-Firestop
    2 × 10 @ 16" O.C.
9-⅝" GWB on Strapping
10-Pine Trim Typ.
11-2 × 3 Furring w/1½"
    R. I. Between
12-6 Mil VB
13-⅝" GWB
14-12 × 12 T.C. Tile
15-4" Conc. Slab
16-2" R. I.
17-6 Mil VB
18-8" Compacted Gravel
19-2 × 12 @ 24" O.C.
20-9" Batt (R—30)

21-1 × 3 Roofers
22-Cedar Shingles
23-1" Air Vent w/Insect
    Screen
24-Cedar Trim Typ.
25-1 × 6 Cedar Soffit
26-Stucco Wall System on
    2" Rigid Insul. (R.I.)
27-½" Plywd.
28-Caulk
29-Wood Dbl. Hung
    Window w/⅝" Insul. Gl.
30-Caulk
31-Pressure Treated Sill &
    Sill Sealer Typ.
32-Crushed Stone Perimeter
    to Footing Drain
33-10" Conc. Wall
34-Filter Mat
35-4" PVC Footing Drain
36-10" × 20" Footing

79

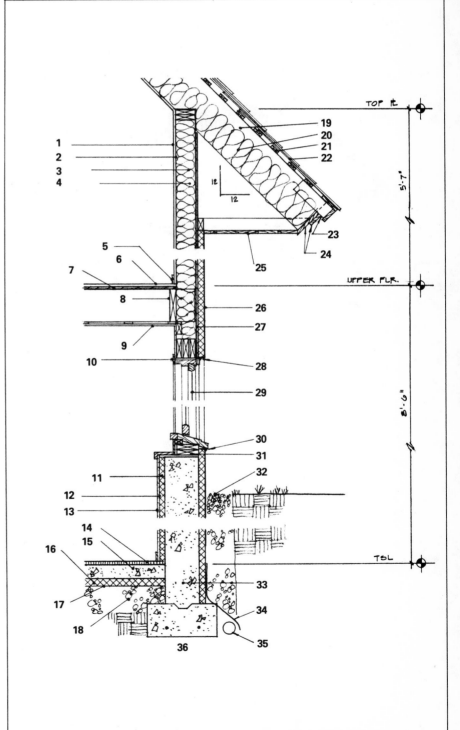

Section AA

Section BB

North

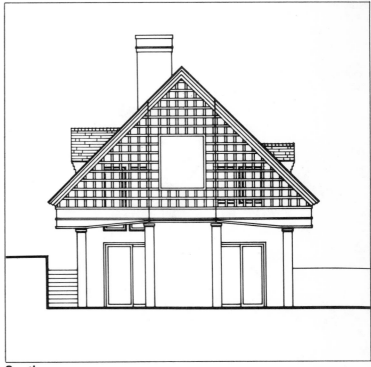

South

East

81

West

Site Plan

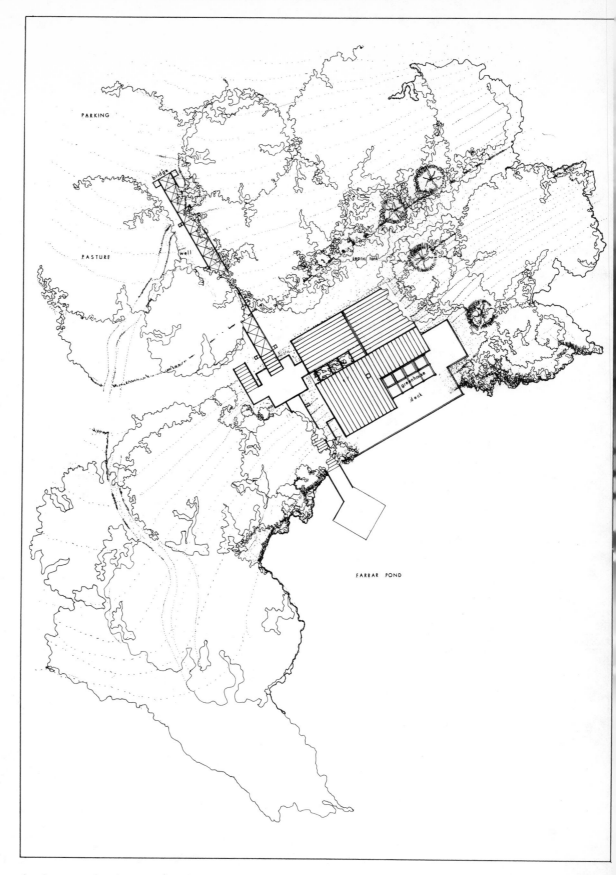

An airy, expansive plan; a
nature-watcher's delight.
Don Metz, judge

Particular considerations
were comfort, the multiple
functioning of space, and an
exploitation of natural site
conditions, all tempered by
a reverence for the topology
and important existing trees.
Kathyanne Cowles, architect

Husher
and Cowles

**Neil Husher and
Kathyanne Cowles**

If you've dreamed of a house built for nature lovers, your dream is answered. Here is your house.

It's designed to fit closely with its surroundings, with its openness, its spacious deck, and its greenhouse.

Children as well as the child in all adults will appreciate this "ultimate treehouse of childhood," as the designers describe it.

By Neil Husher and Kathyanne Cowles

The client is an amateur naturalist who requires a flexible program allowing for both social and solitary usage; here a high, quiet perch provides both and strikes a balance between protection and exposure.

A cost-efficient post foundation emphasizes both long water views and eye-level forest canopy. The house is summer shaded, protected from the northeast winter wind, and well above possible floods.

Passive direct-gain design is complemented by insulated shoji screens to minimize heat loss at night. The client may choose, in cold weather, between the central wood stove or an electric heat pump for primary winter heat. Fans are in place for warm air recirculation, and there is a further client option of adding black metal water drums for heat storage inside the greenhouse.

Particular considerations were comfort, the multiple functioning of space, and an exploitation of natural site conditions, all tempered by a reverence for the topology and important existing trees.

A large planned woodlot will thin over time to grazing land, retaining all trees along the water line and enough growth elsewhere for windbreaks, animal shade, and erosion control.

The parti points not just to a structure in harmony with the terrain, but also to the ultimate treehouse of childhood, reinterpreted according to adult needs.

A long bridge from the driveway/parking area is playful in its suggestion of a moat, but quite serious in its practical linking with the pond below. The ample porch is balanced by a private deck off to the side, designed specifically as a retreat and as a site for a small, protected aviary.

The site is a mixture of meadow, marsh, and woodland on glacial till. The pond shore is either under conservation or in limited private hands dedicated to preservation. The pond supports much migratory and permanent wildlife, and is a routine nesting ground for geese, heron, duck, and osprey.

Technical Data
Project
A Boreal Retreat
Gross square feet
960
Location
Lincoln, Massachusetts
6,400 degree days
Elevation, 130 feet

Materials
Post foundation, post and beam/platform framing, white cedar tongue-and-groove siding, standing seam metal roof, metal grill deck, painted plywood underside, and prefabricated greenhouse

Type
Passive solar, direct gain; superinsulated

Section AA

Section BB

Floor Plan

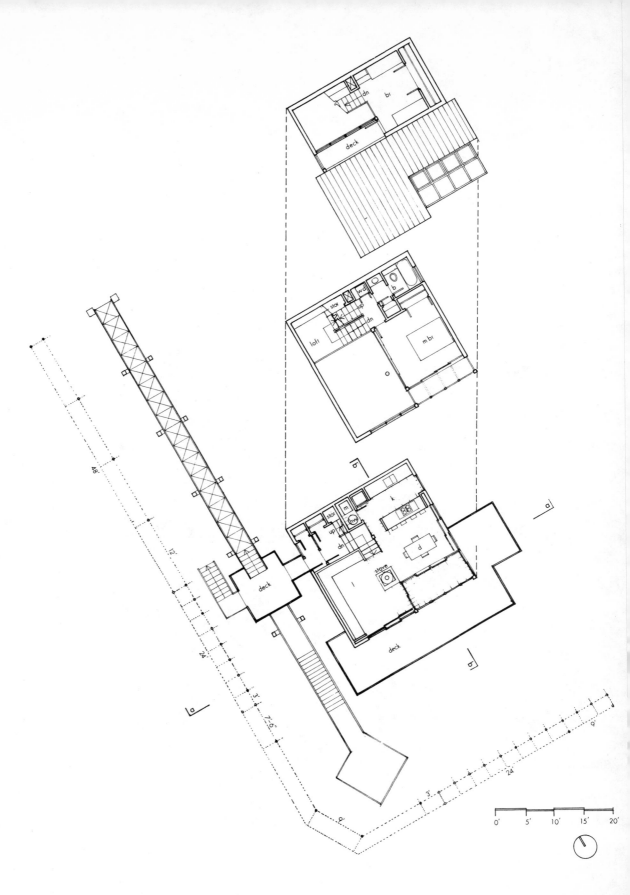

Perspective

Wall Section

1-Standing Seam Metal Roof
2-2 × 12 Rafters @ 24" O.C.
3-10" Batt Insulation
4-1" Foam Insulation Taped For Vapor Barrier
5-Flash
6-Vent Holes
7-Tongue & Groove Siding
8-Wood Deck on Built-up Roof
9-8" Batt Insulation
10-1" Foam Insulation Taped For Vapor Barrier
11-2 × 8 Joists @ 24" O.C.
12-5" Batt Insulation
13-1" Foam Insulation Taped For Vapor Barrier
14-2 × 6 Studs @ 24" O.C.
15-½" CDX Plywood
16-Tongue & Groove Siding
17-Vapor Barrier
18-2 × 12 Joists @ 24" O.C.
19-10" Batt Insulation
20-Wire Mesh
21-4, 2 × 12 Built-up Beams Bolted to Post
22-18" Pressure-Treated Pole (creosote), Notched to Receive Wood Beams
23-Concrete Footing
24-Standing Seam Metal Roof
25-10" Batt Insulation
26-Insulated Shoji Screens
27-Wood Frame Window Fixed Glass, Double Glazed
28-Aluminum Frame Double-Glazed Sliding Glass Doors
29-Insulated Shoji Screens
30-Metal Grill Decking on Pad
31-½" CC Plugged Ext. Plywood Painted
32-18" Pole
33-Steel Cable Cross-Bracing

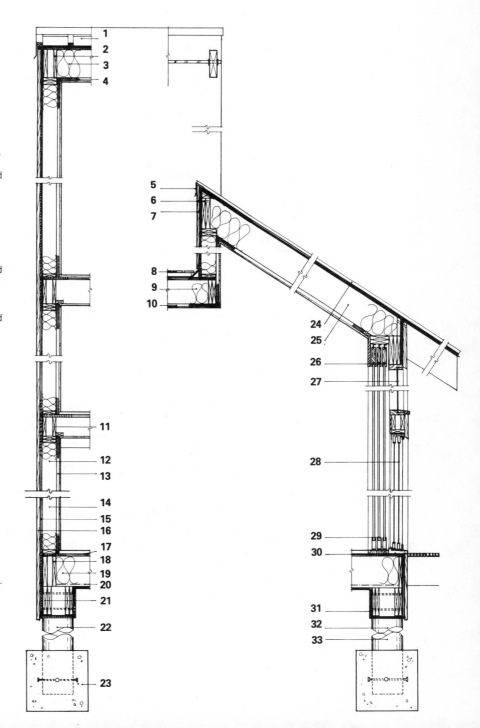

Perspective

This excellent set of plan decisions makes the most of limited space. There's a good understanding of solar potential. Here's a serious effort to find an economical and practical solution to the problems of compact houses.
Don Watson, judge

This house, which is designed to be easily framed with standard materials, has an exposed plank-and-beam ceiling on the first floor, and a metal roof.
Tullio Inglese, designer

Inglese

Tullio Inglese

This house is designed to conserve heat, and does so successfully.

It achieves this without imparting a closed-in feeling, with the south-facing window areas, the skylights, and the first-floor open areas helping to avoid it.

By Tullio Inglese

The Lord House is designed for a lightly wooded lot with a southwesterly slope and view of cornfields beyond. It is a compact two-story cape elongated along its east-west axis for increased winter insulation. The house is purposely designed to reduce foundation and roof areas and, subsequently, to optimize its surface-to-volume ratio. Most closets, entry, utility room, and shelves are located on the exterior wall for added insulation.

The entry, a distinct air lock with entrance door facing east, is at the lowest level, thus preventing cold air from cascading into and through the house.

The kitchen, dining, and living areas revolve clockwise, east-south-west, respectively, around a centrally located wood stove. This placement, and that of the bedrooms, bath, and laundry, is in direct response to our client's program and to specific site conditions including approach from the road, solar access, privacy, views, and winter and summer prevailing winds.

Heat Production and Distribution
1. Winter solar gain through vertical south glass.
2. Centrally located wood stove.
3. Heat pump with independent air handler to de-stratify and distribute air to all rooms.

Heat Retention
1. Well-insulated walls (R-30), ceilings (R-40), and floors (R-14).
2. Dark ceramic tile on first-floor concrete slab.
3. Brick chimney mass and concrete steps near wood stove.
4. Two water columns.
5. ⅝-inch gypsum board (not in contact with studs).
6. Storm windows with insulated (R-8) shades.
7. Earth berm with coniferous trees on north.

Cooling
1. Heat pump.
2. Continuous soffit vents and gable vents.
3. Thermal mass.
4. Well-insulated envelope.
5. Deciduous trees on south and west.
6. Window shades.

The house, which is designed to be easily framed with standard material, has an exposed plank-and-beam ceiling on the first floor, and a metal roof.

Technical Data
Project
Betty Lord House
Gross square feet
1,000
Location
Burlington, Iowa
6,101 degree days
Elevation, 650 feet

Materials
Wood
Type
Passive solar

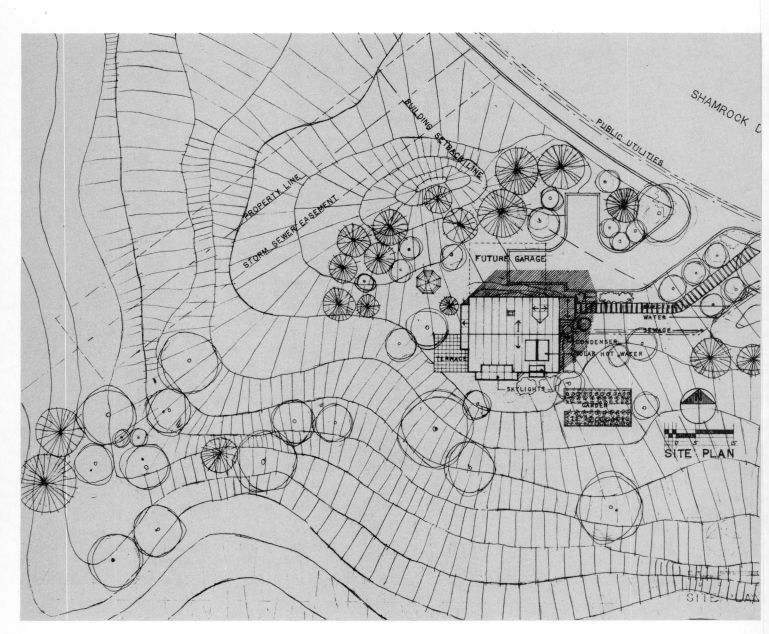

Site Plan

Wall Section

1-2 × 8 Rafters at 2'–0"
   O.C.
2-12" Fiberglass
3-Air Space
4-⅝" CDX Plywood
5-15 Lb. Roofing Felt
6-Raised Rib Metal Roof
7-Cedar Trim
8-Continuous Soffit Vent
9-2 × 4 Spacer
10-2 × 6 Studs at 2'–0"
11-1 × 6 Vertical Cedar
   Siding
12-Glass
13-Bay Window Unit
14-Maple Work Shelf
15-½" CDX Plywood
16-6" Fiberglass
17-2 × 6 Sole Plate
18-2 × 6 Sill
19-Waterproofing
20-½"∅ × 12" Anchor Bolt
21-8" Concrete Foundation
22-4" Perforated Drain
23-Continuous Footing
24-4 Mil. Poly. V.B.
25-⅝" Gypsum Board
26-1" Rigid Insulation
27-2 2 × 6 Plates
28-Painted Pine B.B.
29-1 × 6 T&G Yellow Pine
30-½" Sound Board
31-2 × 6 T&G Planks
32-4 × 8 Douglas Fir 4' O.C.
33-Painted Pine Trim
34-1" Rigid Insulation
35-4 Mil. Poly. V.B.
36-⅝" Gypsum Board
37-1 × 4 Painted Pine
   Baseboard
38-Ceramic Tile
39-5" Concrete Slab
40-2" Rigid Insulation
41-4 Mil Poly. V.B.
42-Compacted Gravel
43-2" Rigid Insulation

91

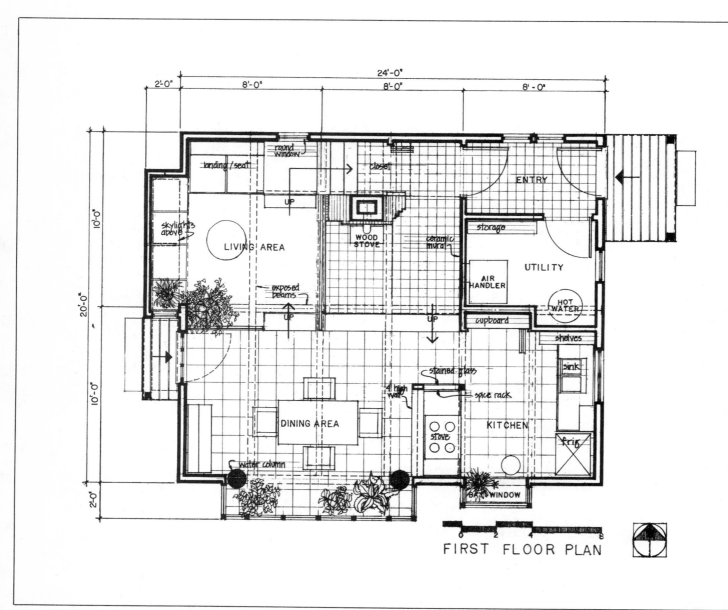

24'-0"

2'-0"   8'-0"   8'-0"   8'-0"

landing / seat   round window   closet   ENTRY
UP
skylights above   storage
LIVING AREA   WOOD STOVE   ceramic mural   UTILITY
AIR HANDLER
10'-0"
exposed beams   UP   HOT WATER
UP   cupboard
shelves
20'-0"   UP
sink
stained glass
spice rack
4' high wall   KITCHEN   frig
10'-0"   DINING AREA   stove
water column
2'-0"   BAY WINDOW

0   2   4   8

FIRST FLOOR PLAN

First Floor Plan

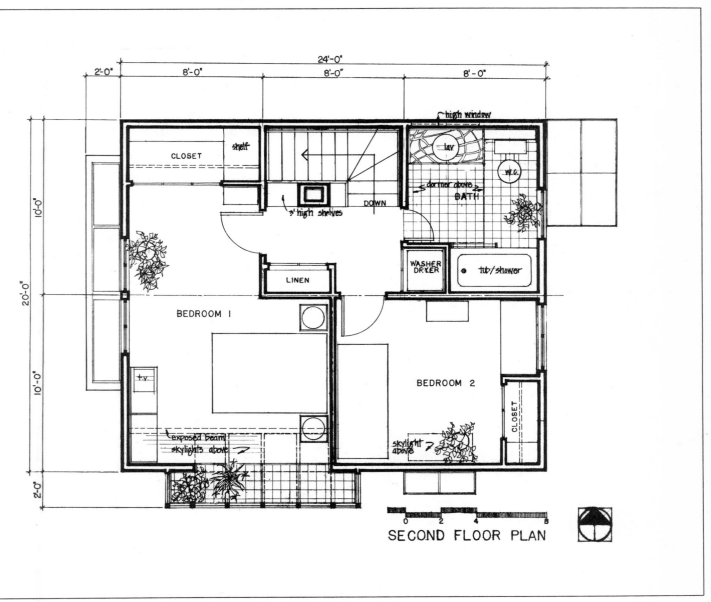

24'-0"

2'-0" 8'-0" 8'-0" 8'-0"

high window

10'-0"

CLOSET shelf lav

DOWN dormer above
BATH W.C.

3' high shelves

20'-0" LINEN WASHER
DRYER tub/shower

BEDROOM 1

10'-0" t.v. BEDROOM 2 CLOSET

exposed beam
skylights above skylight
above

2'-0"

0 2 4 8

SECOND FLOOR PLAN

Perspective

Very expensive to build.
Ralph Johnson, judge

The design is adaptable to
various site conditions,
climates, and alternate
lifestyles.
Edward M. Jones, architect

Jones

Edward Madison Jones

Two models, each with a different floor plan, are offered with this design. One is for a suburban setting, the other for a rural area with a far greater demand for energy efficiency.

The basic design of the house area is a square, with one triangular half a sunken garden, the other an earth-sheltered house, protected by a south-sloping hill.

By Edward Madison Jones

The intent of this concept is to create an efficient, quality, garden environment that is adaptable to many different site conditions and family lifestyles, and is economical to build and operate.

A reevaluation of architectural standards relative to conventional family needs was necessary to reduce space requirements while increasing spaciousness.

A reevaluation of residential form was necessary to integrate passive solar heating and cooling techniques while maintaining orientation flexibility.

A passive solar direct heat gain technique utilizes the sunken garden, floor-to-ceiling double-glazed glass, and the triple-glazed skylight. During the winter, when the tree has lost its leaves, the protected garden becomes a heat sink, which increases the outside temperature adjacent to the glass wall, thereby reducing interior heat loss.

Direct solar energy enters the house through the glass wall and skylight. It is stored in the exposed floor slab and rear wall mass. Cooler room temperatures cause the stored heat to radiate back into the interior.

The centrally located fireplace is actually a high efficiency wood-burning stove with glass screens, outside combustion air intakes, and an air chamber built into the hood. With the barometric evaporative cooler damper closed, the air inside the chamber is heated quickly by the fire and is drawn through the exposed sculptural duct system by natural convection. In-line duct "assist" fans could be incorporated to accelerate air movement when necessary.

Wind power could supply electrical energy for auxiliary portable floor units when more heat is needed. The pole fan above the sleeping loft provides additional warm air circulation.

For cooling, the garden tree and canvas trellis shade flush south glazing without inhibiting the view, and the five-foot porch overhang protects living room glass. A removable wooden lattice screen is placed over the skylight to minimize direct solar exposure, and the earth-insulated wall stabilizes exterior wall temperatures.

Technical Data
Project
Christopher House
Gross square feet
1,000

Location
Rural: Prescott, Arizona
4,782 degree days
Elevation, 5,354 feet
Suburban: Phoenix, Arizona
1,765 degree days
Elevation, 1,033 feet

Materials
Rural: earth, cast-in-place sand-blasted concrete retaining walls, precast concrete roof, slab panels
Suburban: earth, sand-blasted concrete masonry unit retaining walls, timber roof structure, metal cladding

Type
Earth-integrated, hybrid passive solar

95

The garden micro-climate, humidified by the foundation, produces cooler air during the warmer months. It is drawn into the house through the two sliding doors. Natural convection is created by the opened skylight and is augmented by the pole fan.

During the cooling mode, the evaporative cooler, shaded by the vertically extended fireplace walls, force air into the hood air chamber and through the duct system, pressurized by opposed blade dampers located in the supply pipes.

Site Plan

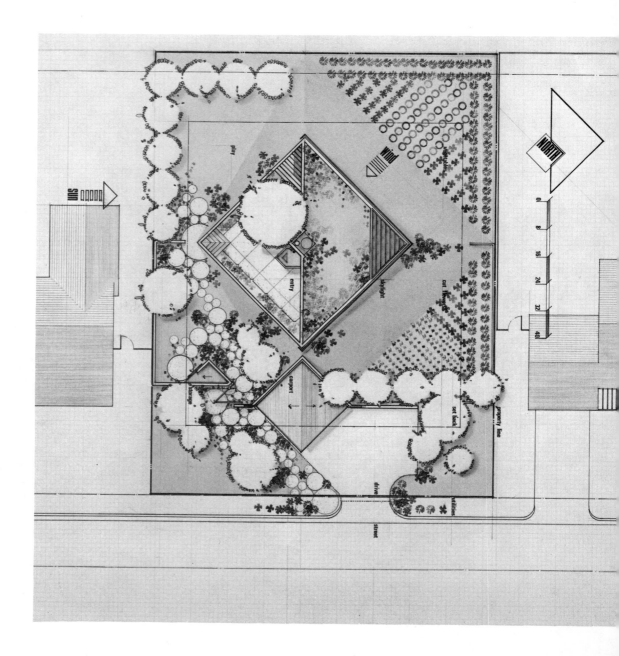

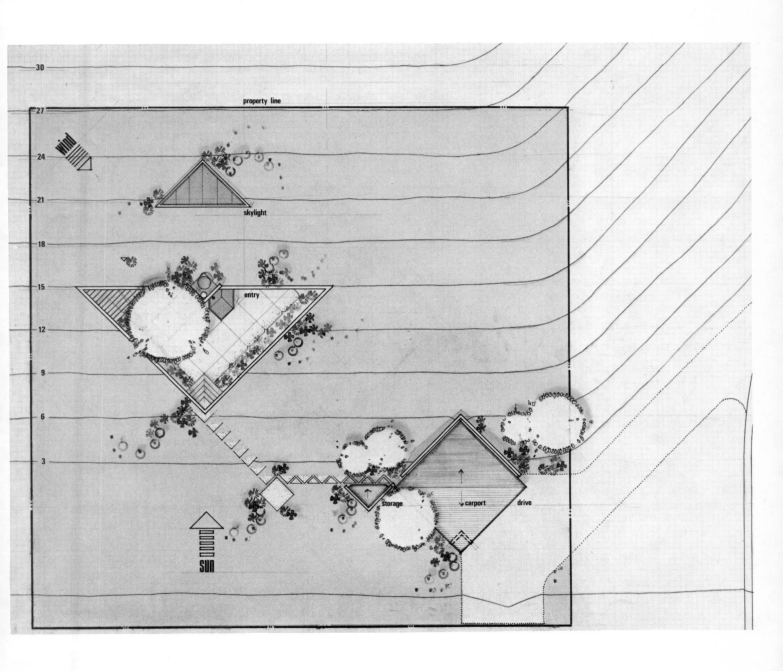

30

property line

27

wind

24

21

skylight

18

15

entry

12

9

6

3

SUN

storage

carport

drive

97

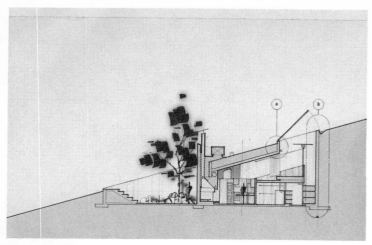

Section AA

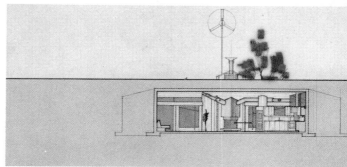

Section BB

MAIN LEVEL

- bedroom 2
- stor
- bath
- vanity
- dining
- kitchen
- laun
- fp
- living/sleep
- entry
- mech stor
- garden
- 44'-0 sq
- u
- c

CEILING LEVEL

- sleeping loft
- hwt
- upper living

NORTH

0   8   16   24

Floor Plan

98

ection CC

Section DD

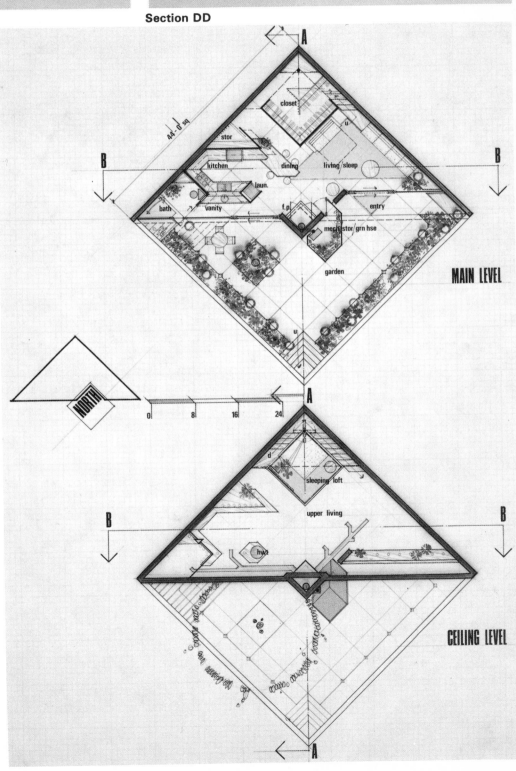

closet

stor

kitchen

dining

living/sleep

laun.

bath

vanity

f.p.

entry

mech/stor/grn hse

garden

44'-0 sq

MAIN LEVEL

NORTH

0   8   16   24

sleeping loft

upper living

hwt

CEILING LEVEL

Floor Plan

99

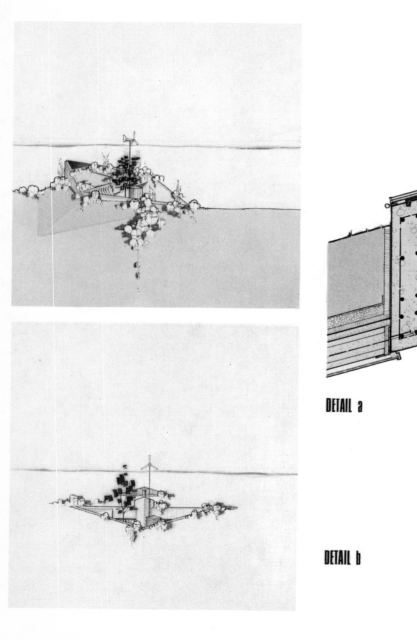

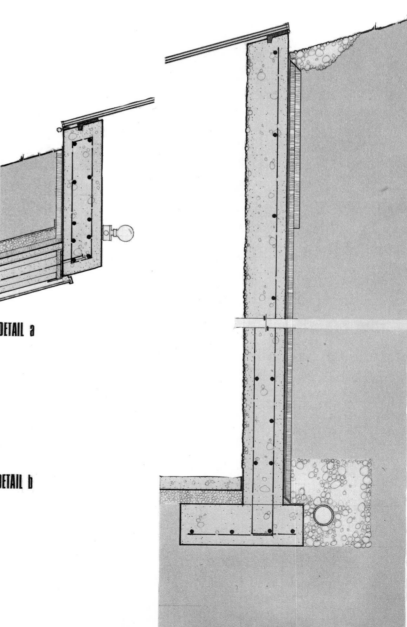

DETAIL a

DETAIL b

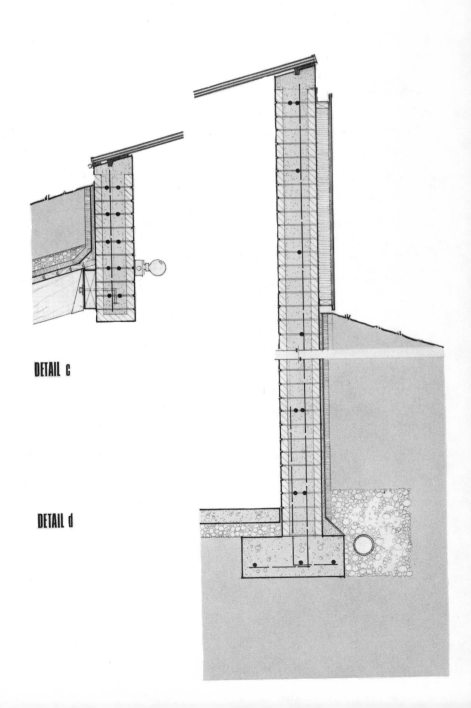

DETAIL c

DETAIL d

Perspective

One big space—great.
Don Metz, judge

It's very simple.
Barry Berkus, judge

The major emphasis of this
house is on the integration
of direct gain passive solar
elements into a simple,
open design.
Keith Krolak, designer

102

Krolak

Keith Krolak
Design Consultant:
Victor Regnier

This house is designed to get the most heat from a passive solar system, and not let that heat leak out in costly amounts.

It's designed, too, with an open interior, contradicting the belief that many small houses, and particularly those with passive solar systems, tend to be cramped. The greenhouse; placement of the stairs; and open arrangement of kitchen, dining, and living areas all contribute to the sense of spaciousness.

By Keith Krolak

The major emphasis of this house is on the integration of direct gain passive solar elements into a simple, open design. Wooden louvers fixed at the appropriate solar angle (in this case, 29°) allow insolation to both the masonry wall and the ceramic tiled ground floor surface.

A greenhouse on the south side provides a collector of solar heat for the masonry thermal storage wall. Retractable insulation may be used to retain heat within the interior glazed areas and skylights.

Basically open, the ground floor plan incorporates an airlock entry where one becomes immediately aware of the inner wall angle canted to provide an interesting hierarchy of living space in relation to the kitchen/dining area, as well as a visible block to the mechanical and storage spaces.

Upstairs bedrooms are open to high spaces and double as studio/loft areas. The garage is optional.

The triangular, single-family zoned site in southwest Champaign is complete with gas, electric, water, and sewage hook-ups. Views are minimal—a house to the distant south and several condominiums and tennis courts to the southwest allow adequate opportunity for a passive solar residence. Breezes prevail from the southwest in summer and northeast in winter. No trees or significant changes in contour currently exist. Complete landscaping would be provided after construction. Roof pitches are set at 45° for possible addition of active solar panels.

Technical Data
Project
Direct Gain Compact House
Gross square feet
988
Location
Champaign, Illinois
5,600 degree days
Materials
Wood with wood siding or brick veneer

Type
Passive solar, double insulated, wood frame construction

Section AA

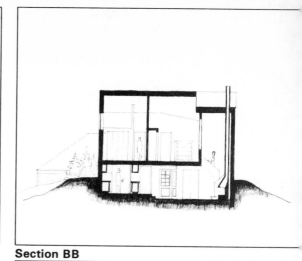

Section BB

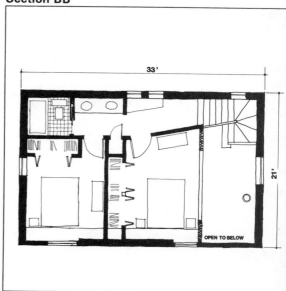

33'

21'

OPEN TO BELOW

First Floor Plan

Second Floor Plan

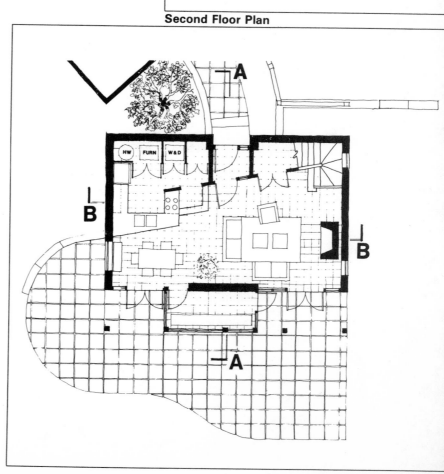

A

HW FURN W&D

B

B

A

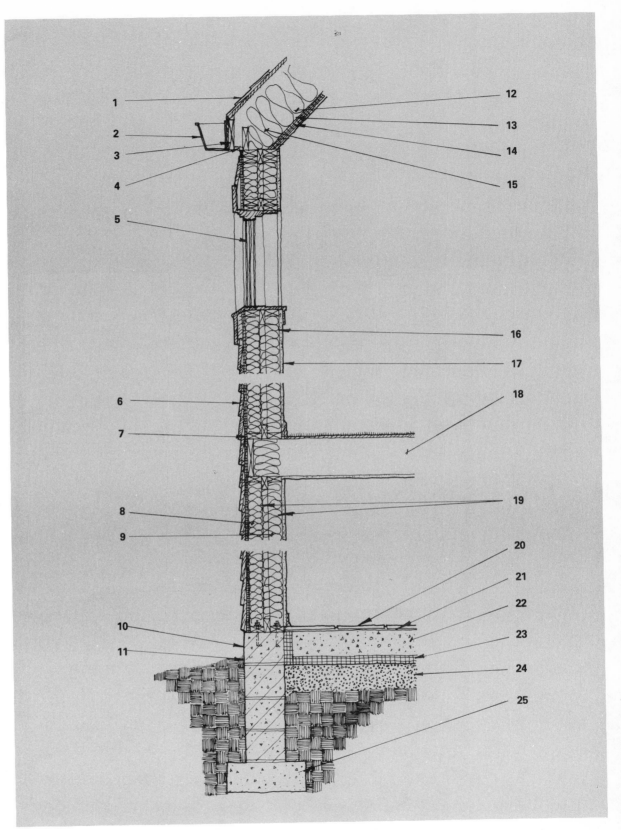

1-Asphalt Shingles
2-Metal Gutter
3-2 × 8 Header
4-Continuous Ridge Vent
5-Triple Glazed Window
 Unit
6-Wood Siding-6″
 Exposure
7-⅝″ Sheathing
8-4″ Batt Insul.
9-6″ Batt Insul.

10-10″ CMU
11-Sealant
12-2 × 12 Roof Joist
13-Vapor Barrier
14-1″ Sheathing
15-10″ Batt Insul.
16-Vapor Barrier
17-½″ Dry Wall
18-2 × 10 Floor Joist
19-Double Insulated Wall
 2 × 4 Studs 24″O.C.

20-Ceramic Tile
21-Mortar
22-6″ Conc. Slab w/6″ Wire
 Mesh
23-2″ Rigid Insul.
24-6″ Gravel Fill
25-Conc. Footing

Perspective

Simple, elegant, economical, adaptable to most climates.
John Hix, judge

Real simple. A real classic. Why make it any more complicated than it needs to be? I like it.
Don Metz, judge

The compact house would be an economic alternative to the mobile home.
Tom Leytham, architect

Leytham

Tom Leytham

This house is designed for the often hostile winter weather of Vermont.

Tom Leytham placed the house on a site sheltered from the worst of winter's winds, but open—and receptive—to the sunshine. He insulated heavily. Finally, he planned it so the winter's supply of wood— two cords—is right outside the door, roofed over to shelter it but in the sunshine to promote drying. Those who dwell in this house will thank him for that. It means they can dash out for a day's supply of wood without bundling up or putting on heavy boots.

By Tom Leytham

The compact house should be an economic alternative to the mobile home. To compete, all systems must be based on standard building procedures, and easily constructed by a carpenter or owner-builder.

The heat storage system utilizes the first floor for a collector and storage for both passive solar and wood heat.

This house is in a central Vermont valley with western hills obstructing the afternoon sun. The soil is sandy, providing good septage, but a town system is nearby, and alternative pricing should be considered.

Considerable cost savings could be realized with alternate floor and siding finishes, and altering the heat storage.

Technical Data
Project
Compact House
Gross square feet
993
Location
Central Vermont
8,200 degree days
Elevation, 960 feet

Construction
Slab on grade with light wood frame
Type
Passive solar with wood back-up

107

Floor Plans

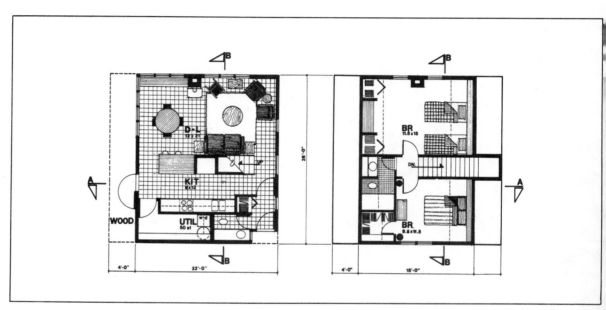

Site Plan

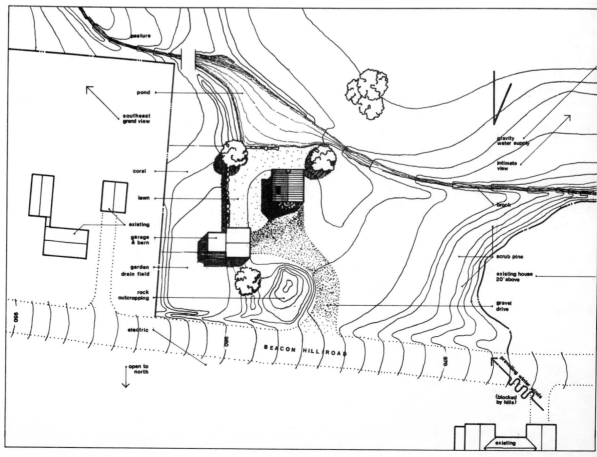

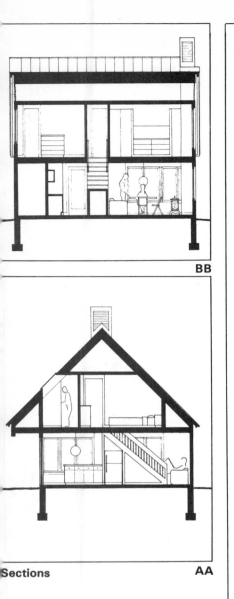

Sections

BB

AA

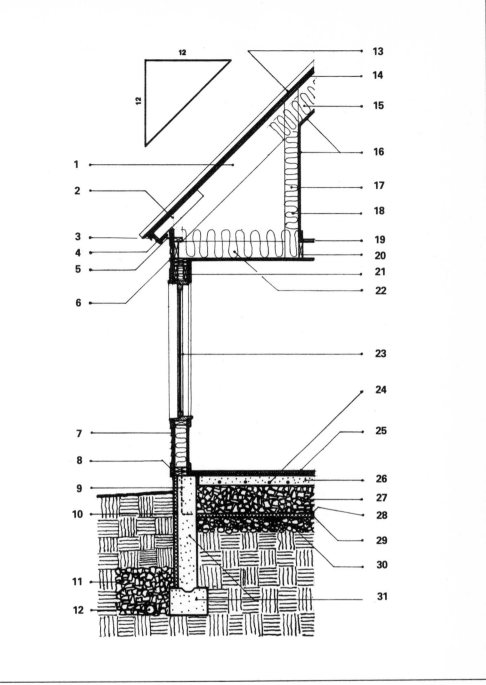

Wall Section

1-2 × 12s – 16″O.C.
2-2 × 4 Scab
3-1 × 2 Trim
4-1 × 6 Trim
5-Eave Vent with Screen
6-Clapboard Siding
7-Insulating Sheathing (Brace)
8-Fiberglass Sill Seal
9-Anchor Bolt
10-2″ Rigid Insulation
11-Crushed Stone
12-Footing Drain
13-Standing Seam Metal Roofing
14-⅝″ Plywood
15-9″ Fiberglass in Sloped Roof and 12″ in Flat
16-Gypsum Board
17-5½″ Fiberglass Insulation with Vapor Barrier
18-2 × 6s – 16″O.C. (Balloon Frame)

19-¾″ Tongue & Groove Plyw'd
20-2 × 10 Blocking
21-2-2 × 6s
22-2 × 10′-16″O.C.
23-Casement Window
24-Heat Piping
25-Masonry Floor Set in Cement Bed
26-Light Weight Concrete Slab
27-Crushed Stone
28-Vapor Barrier
29-2″ Rigid Insulation
30-Gravel
31-Concrete Footing & Frost Wall

Perspective

Has a nice thatch-roof, storybook-cottage feeling combined with the advantages of positive solar potential. Could use some shading devices for summertime comfort.
Don Metz, judge

This compact house design combines simple structural and energy-efficient planning with the detail and craftsmanship of traditional New England building.
William Maclay, architect/planner

110

Maclay

There's a feel of New England about this house, the feel of economy, that a Btu saved is a Btu earned.

While this house offers passive solar possibilities, it concentrates on conserving heat. In a climate that shivers through 8,000 degree days per winter, the (1982) price of heat for this house is estimated at a bargain $150 (wood) or $200 (electricity).

By William Maclay

This compact house design combines simple structural and energy-efficient planning with the detail and craftsmanship of traditional New England building. A regional approach incorporates indigenous forms such as the breezeway, ellipse-shaped and engaged fan trim, and crafted details within a curved roof form. This house design is oriented towards people desiring design and craftsmanship with quality and character. The orientation of the gable end to the south allows for the maximum visual impact by this small house. The elongation of the plan maximizes the solar potential. Options include: earth berming with second-floor entry, garage, breezeway, greenhouse, alternate northwest entry, and attic expansion space.

Given New England's cold, cloudy climate, energy conservation through superinsulated and low infiltration design is cost-effective and necessary. This design utilizes such energy conserving techniques as: space planning oriented to solar access, a continuous vapor barrier with no electrical penetrations, a double airlock entry, triple glazing, R-33 walls, R-38 ceiling, R-15 foundation insulation, and continuous exterior rigid insulation from the foundation through exterior frame walls. The heavy use of insulation reduces the design heat loss to less than 16,000 Btu/h in New England.

The combination of superinsulation and solar contributions will reduce overall energy consumption to less than one or two cords of wood per year, depending on location and user characteristics. If electricity is utilized as the primary heating source, 4,000 kwh of electricity will be used at an annual cost of $200, assuming rates of $0.05 per kilowatt hour. Adequate heat storage is provided in the floor slab and in the overall building materials. Operable windows provide adequate summer cooling.

In addition to solar energy, a wood stove is the main supplementary heat source. Either an instantaneous gas hot water heater used for domestic hot water or an electric heater with peak hour controller will provide heat if the house is unoccupied. A Mitsibishi bathroom-sized, air-to-air heat exchanger with humidistat and timer control in the kitchen and bathroom exhausts stale air. A small thermostat-controlled blower located above the stairs moves solar heated air.

The structural concept minimizes material and labor costs through slab-on-grade construction, optimum value engineered and single-span wood frame construction. The 16-foot width requires no internal structural support and significantly simplifies the framing. Exposed floor framing is utilized in the first-floor ceiling.

Technical Data
Project
Affordable Housing
Gross square feet
978
Location
New Haven, Vermont
8,000 degree days
Elevation, 800 feet

Materials
Wood frame
Type
Passive solar, superinsulated

Perspective

**Bermed Site
With Garage**

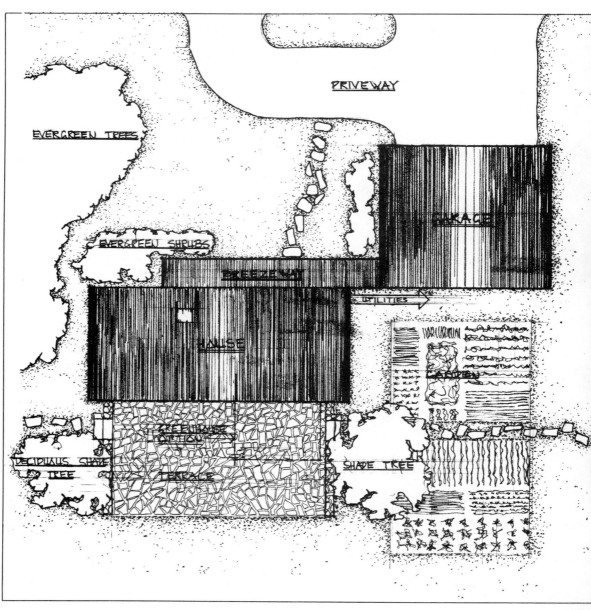

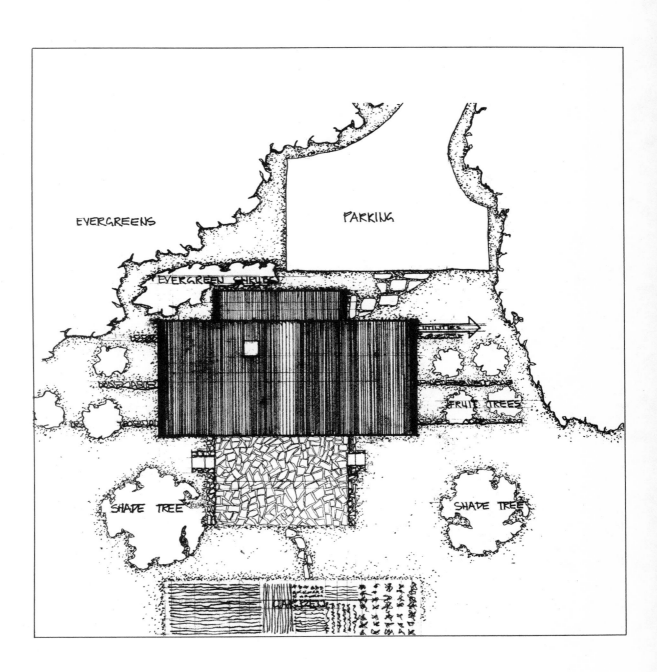

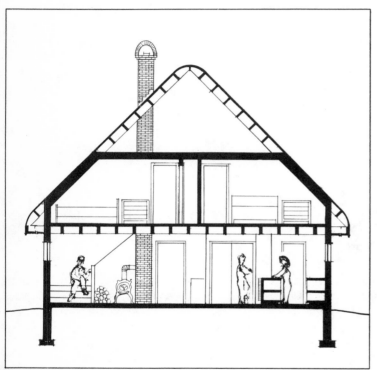

Section AA

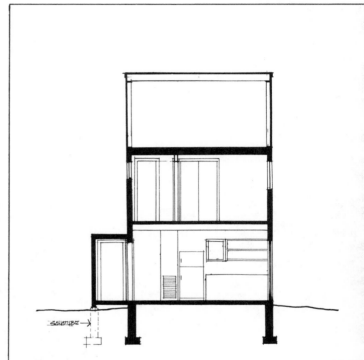

Section BB

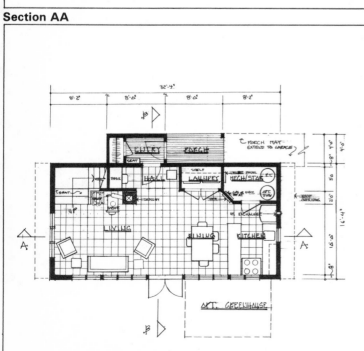

First Floor Plan

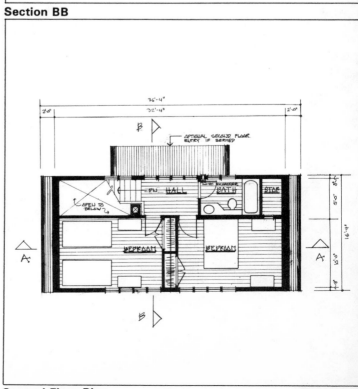

Second Floor Plan

1-Roll Roofing @ Cap
2-15# Felt
3-2 Layers ¼″ AC Ply @
  Curve-Curved Blocking @
  Joints
4-Furring
5-12″ Fiberglass Insulation
6-¾″ Furring-16″O.C.
7-2 × 8 Balloon Framed
  Wall @ East & West
  w/Cont. V.P.
8-Air Space for Elect.
  Chase
9-2 × 6 T&G Flrg.
10-Exposed 4 × 10
  Joists-24″O.C.
11-J or L Bead
12-6 Mil Vapor Barrier w/No
  Penetrations-Lap All
  Joints
13-¾″ Furring for Elect.
  Chase
14-½″ Gyp. Bd.
15-Baseboard
16-½″ Premolded Expansion
  Joint
17-Tile or Slate-Mastic Set
18-1″ EPS Rigid Insulation
19-4″ Slab w/6 × 6 8/8 WW
  Fabric
20-6 Mil Poly-Lap @ Wall
21-Compacted Gravel Fill-4″
  MIU
22-8″ Wall w/2-#4 Bars-Top
  & Bot.
23-PTG w/Key or #14 Stl.
  Dowels-24″O.C. Typ.

24-2 × 12 Rafter-24″O.C.
25-12″ Fiberglass Insulation
26-Air Space for Vent
27-Asphalt Shingles
28-15# Felt
29-½″ CDX Sheathing
30-Furring
31-2 Layers ¼″ AC Ply-
  curved Blocking @ Joints
32-Drip Edge
33-Soffit Vent
34-1″ T&G Soffit or ½″ AC
  Ply
35-No Header @ Window-
  Non Structural Wall
36-Permashield Windows or
  Eq. Seal w/Polycel
  Sealant and Vapor
  Barrier
37-Clapboards-3″ Exposed
38-1″ Blueboard Insulation
39-½″ CDX Ply Sheathing
40-9″ Fiberglass Insulation
41-Sill Insulation
42-Aluminum Flashing to
  1'-0″ B.G.
43-3″ Blueboard to 2'-0″
  B.G.
44-Gravel Fill
45-2″ Blueboard Insulation
46-Crushed Stone
47-Perimeter Drain

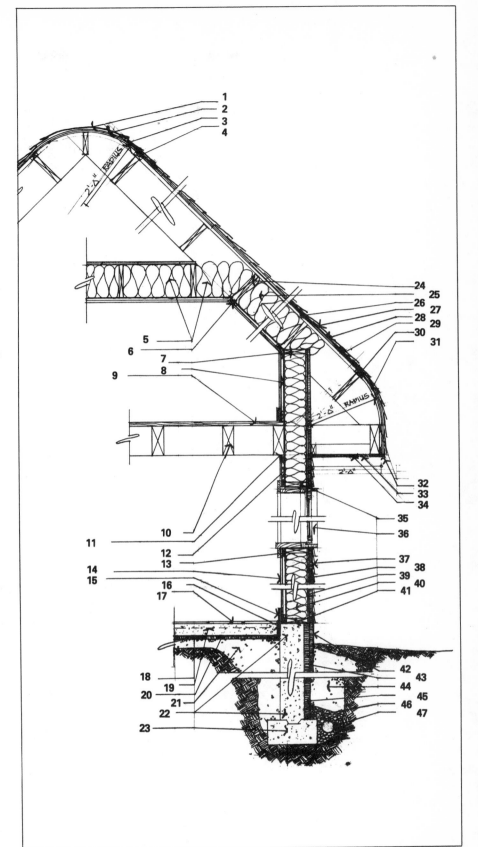

Elevation

Perspective

The plan decisions are sound, dealing with a west view that is site-specific; otherwise the climatic response would be better if the plan were "flipped," with the breakfast room in the east.

Insulating/reflecting panels on the east and west windows are good. The Trombe wall should not require vents. There is a sense of aesthetic control and intent in these drawings.
Don Watson, judge

The styling of this compact house is harmonious with New England residential architecture.
Neil Mongold and Mark Stankard.

Mongold and Stankard

Neil Mongold and
Mark Stankard

Practicality is written into the design of this
house. It makes the most of the square-footage,
and it's built for maximum energy efficiency.

It's one of the least expensive houses in this book,
and one of the cheaper to heat, considering its
New England setting.

By Neil Mongold and Mark Stankard

This compact house is based on square modular geometry and a gabled Trombe wall. To the west of the
house, a grassy meadow falls off toward the Charles
River. The house and garage are positioned to frame
a view of the river on approach. A group of evergreen
trees and the hipped roof protect the house from the
northwest winter winds.

The house is entered through an air lock on axis with
a colored glass block band above the fireplace.

The communal areas of the upper floor are arranged
to be versatile in use and are focused on the Trombe
wall.

A bay window at the stairs illuminates the lower level.
The two bedrooms have ample closet space and windows with solar reflecting/insulating shutters like the
windows above.

All plumbing is stacked on the north side.

The windows and roof are insulated with the Massachusetts climate in mind.

The Trombe wall is divided to heat the upper and lower
levels separately with the same wall-to-floor ratio of
.42/I. Warm air flows over the masonry surface as
well as through the cores filled with river stones. The
fireplace draws on outside air for combustion, and the
flue duct splits to allow the masonry wall to absorb
more heat from the chimney. The back-up system is
an electric forced-air furnace.

The styling of this compact house is harmonious with
New England residential architecture. The building
materials are durable and readily available. The union
of simple building techniques and simple passive solar
technology makes this house efficient and livable.

Technical Data
Project
Compact House in
New England
Gross square feet
1,000
Location
Dover, Massachusetts
5,791 degree days
Elevation, 50 feet

Materials
Wood framing, cedar siding,
concrete block, galvanized
metal roof
Type
Passive solar with enhanced
Trombe wall

Site Plan

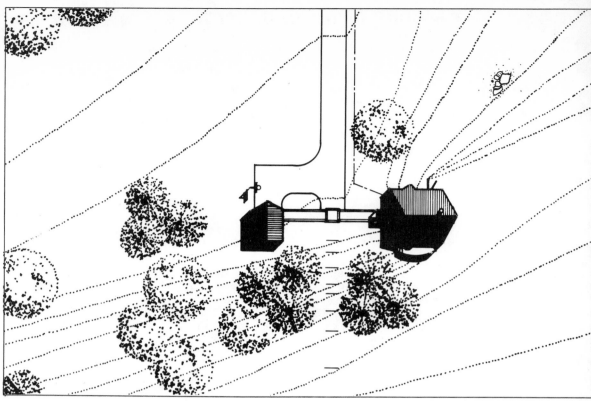

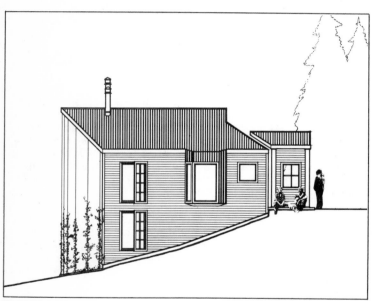

East Elevation

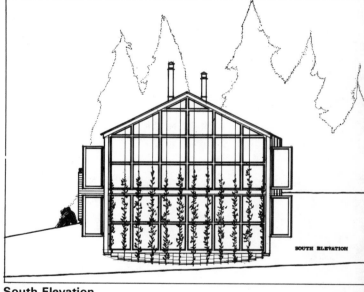

SOUTH ELEVATION

South Elevation

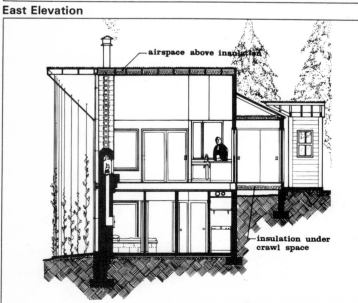

airspace above insulation

insulation under crawl space

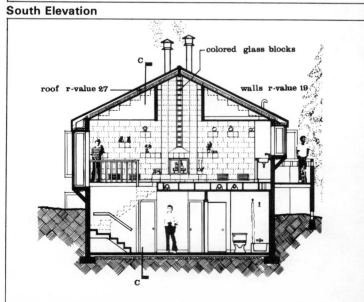

colored glass blocks

roof r-value 27

walls r-value 19

c

c

118

Wall Section

1-Galvanized Metal Chimney
2-Metal Ridge Cap
3-1 × 8 Fascia Board
4-Exterior Grade ½" Plywood Soffit
5-8 Gauge Galvanized Steel Wire
6-Aluminum Mullions Anchored to Masonry with 2" Spacer Bolts
7-Double Glazing
8-Horizontal Wall Reinforcing Trusses Alternate Courses
9-Seasonal Canvas Shading Device
10-Removable Access Panel
11-Reflective Insulating Shades
12-U.V. Resistant Black Stain or Paint
13-Expanded Steel Lath
14-Non-backflow Damper
15-Flashing
16-Concrete Pavers on 4" Gravel
17-Concrete Blocks Grouted Solid
18-1" Rigid Insulation Over Parging and Waterproofing
19-4" Drain Tile
20-Colored Metal Roof on 15# Felts over ½" Plywood Sheathing
21-2 × 8 joists-24"O.C. with 6" Fiberglass Batt Insulation over 1" Rigid Insulation ½" Drywall Ceiling
22-12" Concrete Block Wall with Cores Vertically Aligned and Filled with 2" Riverstones
23-Fireplace
24-2 × 12 Joists 24"O.C. with ¾" Plywood Subfloor under ¾" Finished Wood Floor
25-½" Drywall Ceiling on Furring Strips 16"O.C.
26-Continuous Bond Beam
27-Back-up Heater Duct
28-Optional "Rock Bed" Storage
29-4" Concrete Slab
30-2" Rigid Insulation over 6 Mil. Vapor Barrier on 4" Gravel
31-Compacted Soil
32-12" × 36" Footing with 2 #5 Rebars and 12" Long Dowels 4'-0"O.C.

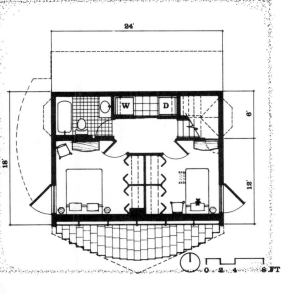

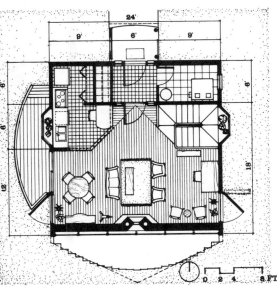

Floor Plans

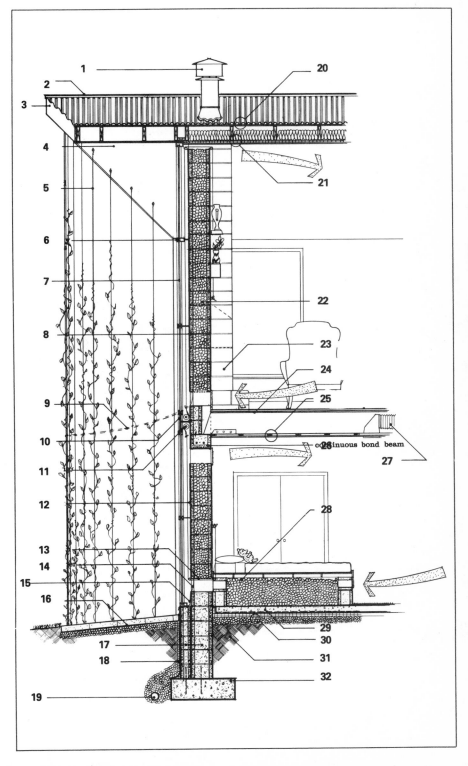

119

Perspective

The organization of the plan, out of the structural module, gives the house coherence and elegance.
Don Watson, judge

By raising the house on a post-and-beam structural system, I have created the flexibility of locating the house on a very steep slope as well as on a flat site.
Mark Nielsen, architect

Nielsen

Mark Jens Nielsen

Mark Jens Nielsen offers a house for a site with a view. In this location, the view is a changing one, a cranberry bog with its varying water levels, its many colors, culminating in bright red in the fall.

The view could be a lake, a mountain, or rolling farmland. Big windows dominate the south side of the house on both levels, promising beauty and sunlight for nearly every room.

The post-and-beam structure sits on a pole foundation, and so can be adapted to any lot, flat or sloping.

The second floor has a master bedroom suite with a study that can be isolated for guests.

The plan calls for electric baseboard heat. But the stove in the center of the living area offers an alternative for those willing to accept the challenges of heating with wood.

By Mark Jens Nielsen

I have chosen the edge of a cranberry bog in Carlisle, Massachusetts, to site this house. This site is unusual, since cranberry bogs provide expansive views, dammed ponds, irrigation canals, and unusual color in the fall before the cranberries are harvested.

The house is oriented a few degrees west of south to take full advantage of the views and southern exposure. The prevailing winds are from the west. The house itself has 85 percent of its glazing on the southern wall, and the remaining 15 percent faces east or west, with no glazing to the north. Heat will be provided by an electric baseboard system, how- ever, by closing the insulative shutters at night and running the wood stove through the winter, the owner can reduce the bill significantly.

By raising the house on a post-and-beam structural system, I have created the flexibility of locating the house on a very steep slope as well as on a flat site. I have added an extra 550 square feet of outdoor storage space, critical to any small house. The cost of footings for posts will be approximately one quarter that of a typical foundation wall and slab. This savings I can invest in custom windows and casement details.

Technical Data
Project
Bog House
Gross square feet
1,000
Location
Carlisle, Massachusetts
5,936 degree days
Elevation, 42 feet

Materials
Wood
Type
Passive solar

121

The plan is straightforward and demonstrates a flexibility in the living area on the first floor and in the
master bedroom/study (guest room) suite on the second floor. The design is a clear structural solution that
lends character and presence to the house, plus a
higher level of detail than is associated with economical houses.

I hope the solution also demonstrates a sensitivity to
traditional New England architecture through its massing, site orientation, economical plan, and materials.

Site Plan

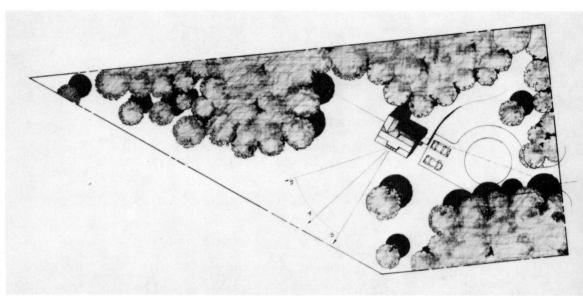

Site Plan

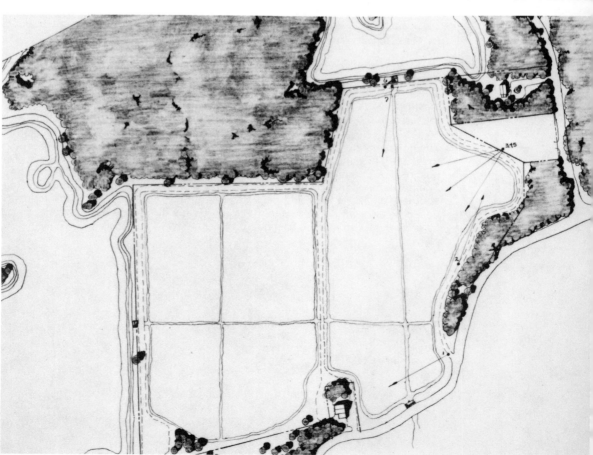

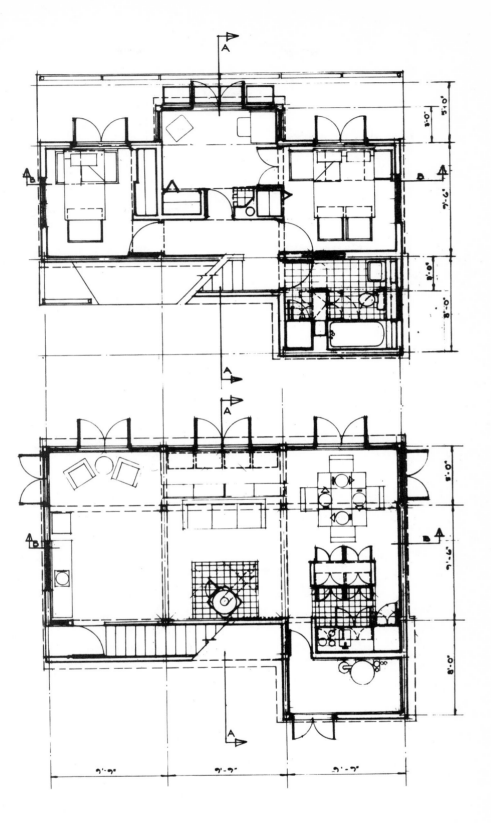

Sections

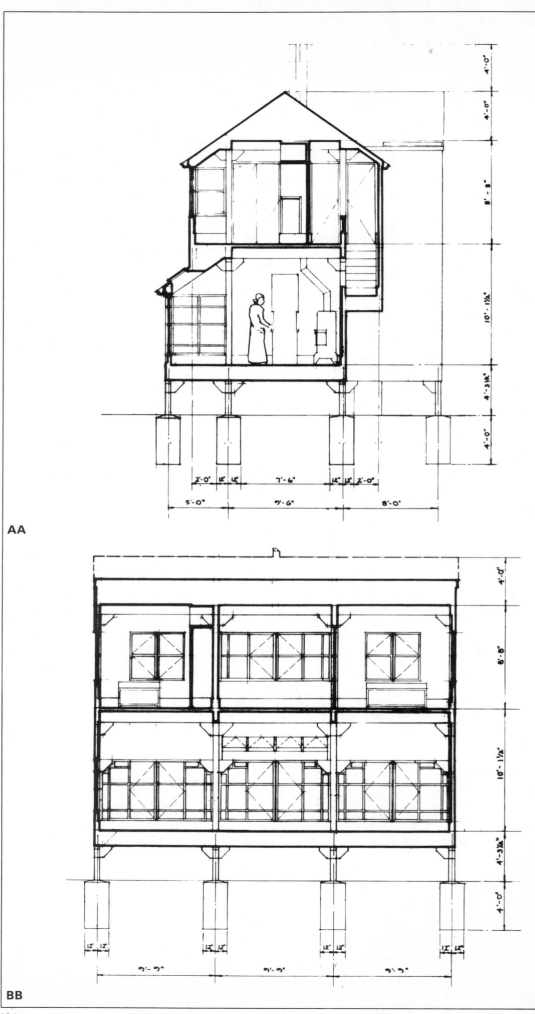

AA

BB

Wall Sections

1-Shingles, Tarpaper & ⅝"
Exterior Grade Plywood

2-2 × 8 Roof Rafters

3-2, 6" Layers of Insulation
or 12" Equ.

4-Vapor Bar.

5-2" Wood Decking T&G

6-6 × 8 Beams

7-Vent Opening w/Bug
Screen

8-Vapor Barrier,
½ Ext. Gr. Ply.
Tarpaper & Clapboards

9-Flashing

10-Double Glazed Windows
Throughout. Not Shown
is the Option of Insulated
Shutters

11-Wood Brace

12-Gyp., Painted ⅝"

13-Electric Heating Unit

14-Hard Wood Flooring

15-3" T&G Wood Deck

16-Flashing

17-Vapor Barrier

18-6 × 10 Wood Beams

19-2 × 6 Rafters w/6"
Insulation

20-1 × 3 Spacers

21-Wood Brace

22-6" Insulation

23-⅝" Ext. Gr. Ply.,
Tarpaper & Asphalt
Shingles

24-1 × 3 Spacers for Venting

25-Vapor Barrier

26-Metal Gutter

27-⅝" Gyp. Paint

28-6 × 8 Wood Beam

29-Shim

30-Trim Piece

31-Vent w/Bug Screen

32-Flashing

33-Insulated Shutters
Ridged Insul. Framed
w/Wood Trim & Covered
w/Cloth

34-Double Glazed Windows

35-Flashing

36-2" Ridged Insulation

37-Electric Heating Element

38-Hardwood Floor w/3"
T&G Decking

39-Flashing

40-Vapor Barrier

41-6 × 12 Wood Beam

42-2 Layers of 6" Insul. or
Equivalent w/V2" Ext.
Gr. Ply. (Vented)

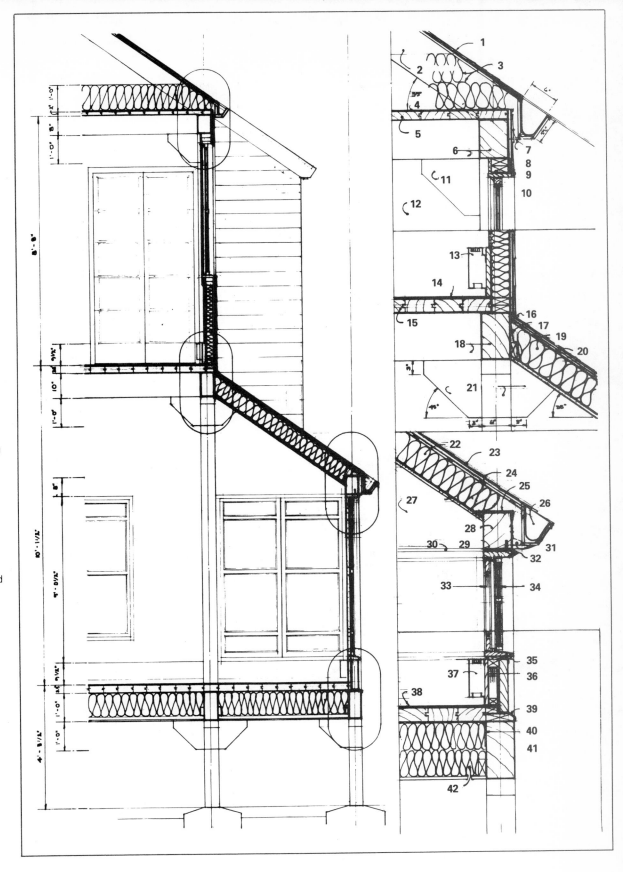

125

Perspective

This project shows a sensitive combination of appropriate technology and good design with a well-ordered range of scale and proportion.
Don Metz, judge

. . . the house is conceived as a modest but comfortable shelter, retreating into itself in cold weather and opening up to the site in warm weather.
Bruce Osen, designer

Osen

Bruce Osen

The Far East in West Virginia?

And why not, if the design is keyed to both the climate of the area and the lifestyle of the homeowners?

Study this house carefully. It has features some would delight in, others might prefer to avoid. The composting toilet, the large area devoted to bath and shower, the k'ang (a raised and heated masonry floor room).

The summer kitchen, a valuable carryover from the past, and the sleeping porch promise comfort for those seeking a simpler way of life. These and the deck offer a spaciousness not expected in fewer than 1,000 square feet of interior space.

By Bruce Osen

The site is a ridge top in Summers County, West Virginia, with excellent views of the New River and the village of Sandstone to the northeast, and tree-covered Chestnut Mountain to the south.

This area has cool winters; pleasant springs and falls; and warm, hazy summers. Annual rainfall is about 35 to 45 inches. The wettest month is July; the driest, October.

Planned for owner-builders, the house is conceived as a modest but comfortable shelter, retreating into itself in cold weather and opening up to the site in warm weather. The overhanging roof not only provides protection for upper-level sleeping porches,

summer kitchen, entry, and north porch, but collects rainwater to be filtered and stored as the primary domestic supply.

Inside the house, storage areas are located on the north, living areas on the south.

The k'ang, or Korean-style heated masonry floor, forms the center of the house. Furniture is kept to a minimum; seating is built in or a function of floor level change.

Folding beds create more usable space upstairs and allow flexibility of sleeping location. Folding chairs and an expandable table provide extra space for dinner guests.

Technical Data
Project
Averill Rossi House
Gross square feet
875, excluding porches
Location
Sandstone, West Virginia
5,190 degree days
Elevation, 1,640 feet
Materials
Masonry, wood

Type
Passive solar with wood heat back-up

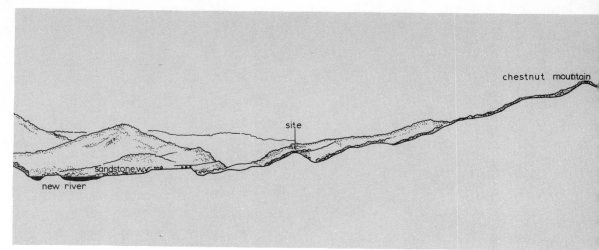

Site Plan

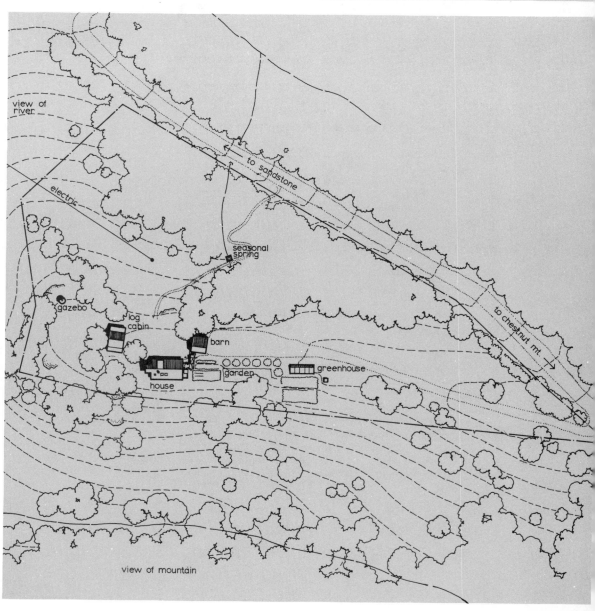

Floor Plans

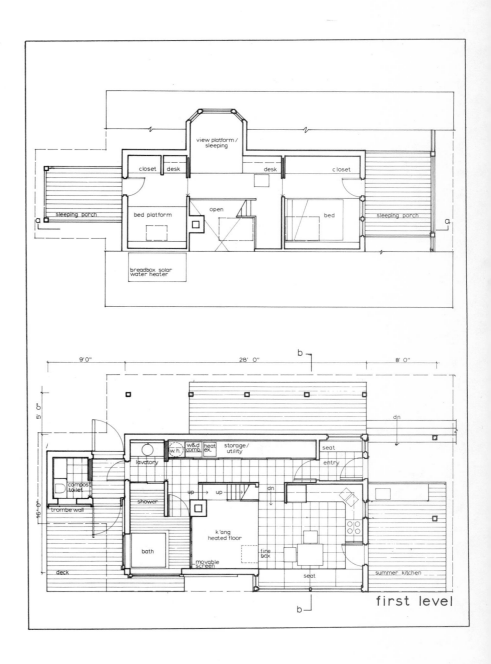

view platform /
sleeping

closet | desk | desk | closet

sleeping porch

bed platform | open | bed | sleeping porch

breadbox solar
water heater

9' 0"   28' 0"   b   8' 0"

5' 0"

dn

16' 0"

w.h. | w&d comb. | heat ex. | storage / utility | seat

lavatory | entry

compost toilet

trombe wall

shower

up | up | dn

deck

bath | k'ang heated floor | fire box

movable screen | seat | summer kitchen

b

first level

Perspective

Section AA

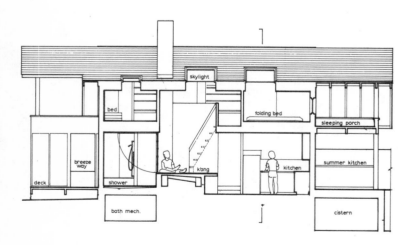

Section BB

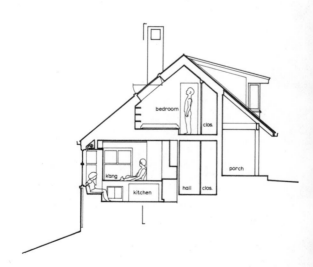

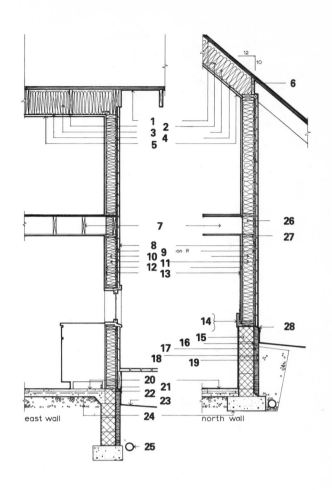

east wall

north wall

Wall Section

1-⅝" CDX Plywood
2-2 × 12" Rafters
3-12" Fiberglass Insulation R-38
4-6 Mil Poly Vapor Barrier
5-½" Drywall
6-Vents
7-2 × 10 Floor Joists
8-1" Drop Siding
9-1" Rigid Insulation R-6.5
10-6" Fiberglass Insulation R-19
11-2 × 6 Studs
12-6 Mil Vapor Barrier
13-½" Drywall
14-Elec. Wiring Where Required on Exterior Walls is Placed in Raceways on the Interior Side of Vapor Barrier

15-Stack Bonded 8" Conc. Block
16-Bentonite Waterproofing
17-2" Rigid Insulation
18-6 Mil Poly
19-Cement Asbestos Board
20-4" Conc. Slab
21-Pressure Treated Sill
22-Sill Sealer
23-Grade
24-6 Mil V B
25-4" Drain
26-North Wall Balloon Framed
27-Firestops
28-Drip Strip/Termite Shield

View from Southeast

The kitchen, although tucked in a corner and somewhat out of sight, is still open to the main activity areas.
J. Douglas Peix and William Crawford, architects

An elegant country cottage with an appealing big-little scale, good zoning, and good planning for expansion.
Don Metz, judge

Peix
and Crawford

**J. Douglas Peix and
William R. Crawford**

While this house is designed specifically for a retired couple, don't pass it by simply because you're decades away from your first Social Security check.

This house has delightful features that will appeal to any age group. One of them is the bridge leading to the bedrooms and separating the two-story dining and living areas. Another is the window seat/bed on the stairway and tucked snugly against the Trombe wall.

The designers have shown how this house can be expanded with the addition of a porch and garage as ells on the east and west sides.

By J. Douglas Peix and William R. Crawford

Approaching the house, the garage and porch suggested in the developed plan stretch across the entry elevation, allowing the house to command an impressive aspect on the landscape. Seen this way, this compact house appears large.

The house is organized with service spaces on the north, sheltering the house and allowing the public rooms facing south to overlook a terrace that leads to an allée of fruit trees and a picturesque view of farmland.

The garage blocks winter winds and directs summer breezes to the house.

House
The double-height living and dining spaces make this compact house feel spacious and open, while the second-floor bridge articulates the space into more intimate functional areas.

The kitchen, although tucked in a corner and somewhat out of sight, is still open to the main activity areas.

The bedrooms also share in the double-height space by having casement windows which can be closed for acoustical privacy.

A window seat on the stair landing doubles as a bed for an extra overnight guest.

Heating
Large south-facing windows permit the sun to warm the black slate floor of the main living spaces; there are no north-facing windows.

With its central location and masonry back wall, the wood stove can heat the entire house.

An air-to-air heat exchanger conserves heat while allowing fresh air to enter the tightly sealed, superinsulated house.

Technical Data
Project
Bridge House, Cottage for a Retired Couple
Gross square feet
997
Location
Malvern, Pennsylvania
4,800 degree days
Elevation, 152 feet

Materials
Cedar clapboards, wood frame structure, asphalt shingle roof, insulation
Type
Superinsulated, assisted passive solar

133

The Trombe tower radiates heat at night and the fan-assist system directs daytime heat to the rock bed for later use.

The Trombe wall and plenum are articulated to illustrate the solar design while expressing them within traditional domestic forms.

Cooling
Deep eaves and shade trees block the summer sun. The vented attic wall reduces heat build-up. Buried air ducts provide earth sink cooling.

All major rooms have cross ventilation.

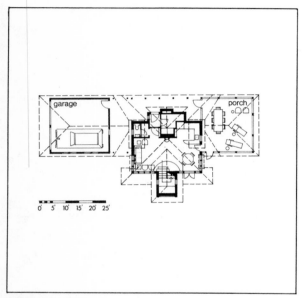

Developed Plan

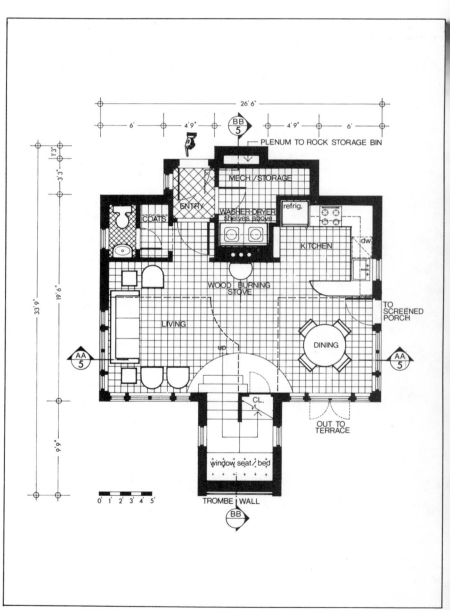

Lower Level Plan

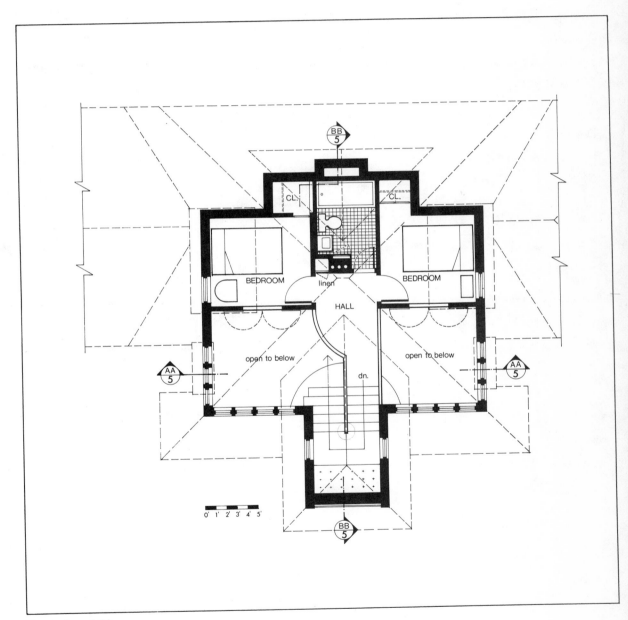

Upper Level Plan

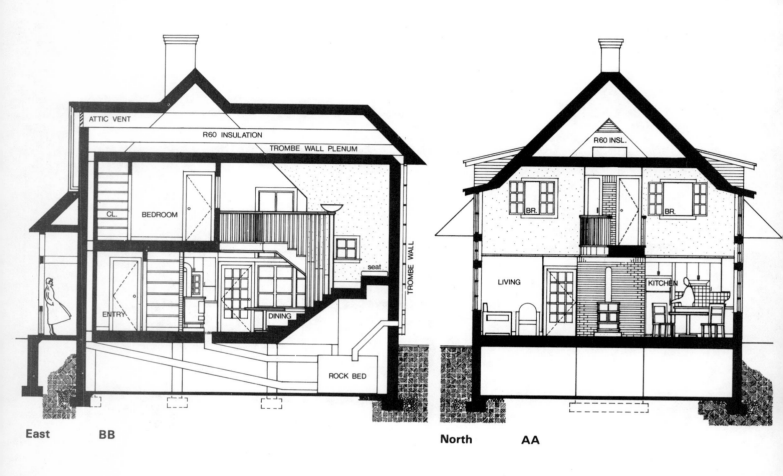

ATTIC VENT

R60 INSULATION

TROMBE WALL PLENUM

CL.

BEDROOM

seat

TROMBE WALL

ENTRY

DINING

ROCK BED

R60 INSL.

BR.

BR.

LIVING

KITCHEN

East   **BB**

North   **AA**

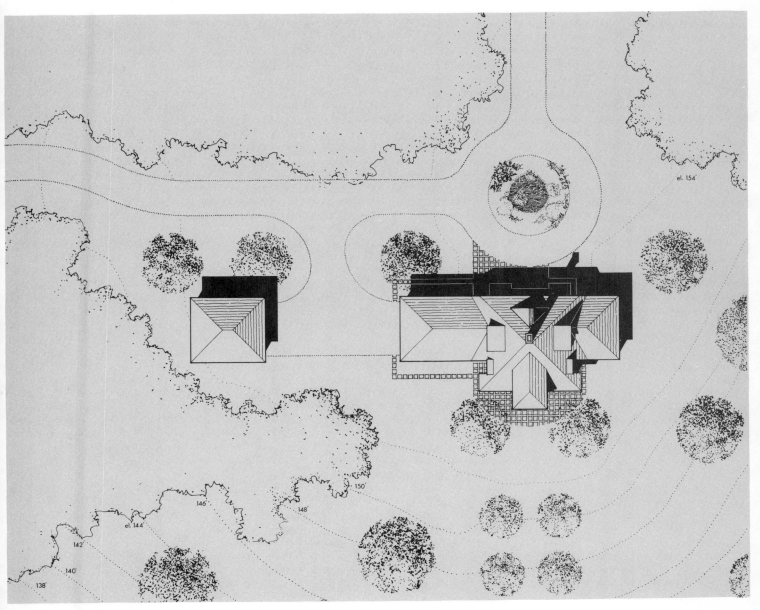

Site Plan

Trombe Wall

1-Inflatable Insulating
  Curtain in Insulated
  Housing
2-Upper Outside Vent
  Continuous Hinge
3-Cedar Face
4-¾" Exterior Plywood
5-1½" Rigid Insulation
6-Insect Screening
  Weather Strip
7-Latch
8-4" Air Space
9-⅝" Tempered Insulating
  Glass
10-Cedar Mullion with
  Removable Stop
11-1 Part Portland Cement,
  1 Part Sand Slurry with
  Black Masonry Pigment
  & Black Concrete Stain
12-Heavy Weight Concrete
  Masonry Unit Grouted
  Solid
13-2 #4 Rebars @ 24"O.C.
14-#4 Rebars @ 16"O.C.
15-Lower Outside Vent
  Similar to Upper Vent
16-Flashing &
  Counterflashing
17-⅜" Diameter Weeps
  2'0"O.C. with Insect
  Screening

18-R-60 Roof Insulation
19-Thermosiphon Plenum
  with Automatic Damper
  to Rock Bed Heat
  Storage
20-2 × 10 Joists
21-R-19 Batt Insulation
  Under Plenum
22-Chicken Wire Support for
  Insulation
23-6 Mil Polyethylene Vapor
  Barrier
24-Painted GWB Laminated
  Directly to Concrete
  Block
25-Typical Wood Floor
26-Back Draft Damper
27-Thermosiphon Loop
  Return
28-R-19 Insulated Crawl
  Space
29-Rock Bed
30-Automatic Damper
31-Sand
32-6 Mil Poly Film
33-R-15 Rigid Insulation
34-¾" Plywood Enclosure
35-Dry, Clean, Non-Radon
  Producing Rocks
36-Metal Lath
37-Concrete Block Plenum
38-¼" Masonite

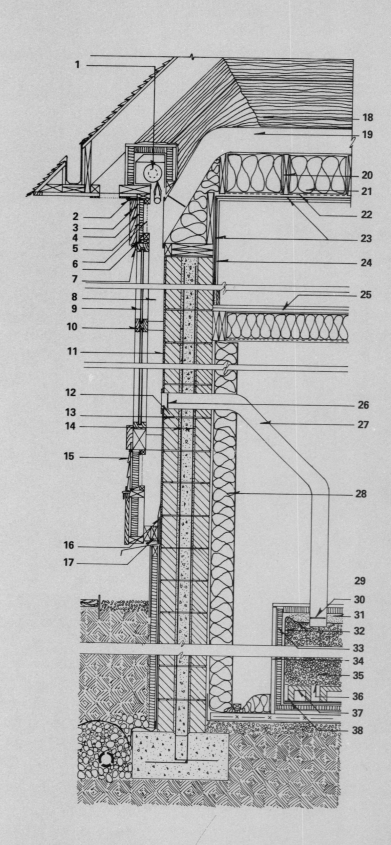

1-Asphalt & Fiberglass Overlay, Fed. Spec. SS-S-001534, Class A, Type I; UL Class A, Over No. 15 Asphalt Saturated Felt; Fasten with Hot Galvanized Steel Roofing Nails

2-Copper Flashing

3-¾" Exterior Grade Plywood Roof Deck

4-Inset Copper Gutter with Flashing & Counterflashing

5-Continuous Eave Roof Vent with Insect Screening

6-2 × 6 Sole Plates

7-2 × 10 Header & Floor Joists

8-2 × 6 Cap Plates

9-2 × 6 Studs, 24"O.C.

10-Flashing

11-Cedar Trim 6" × ¾"

12-Cedar Rabbeted Bevel 5" × ⁹⁄₁₆" Siding

13-½" Exterior Grade Plywood Sheathing

14-1" Tongue & Groove Rigid Polystyrene Sheathing

15-R-19 Batt Insulation

16-1" Rigid Polystyrene Insulation

17-6 Mil Polyethylene Vapor Barrier

18-⅝" Gypsum Wall Board

19-2 × 6 Sole Plates

20-2 × 12 Cedar Trim

21-Copper Shield

22-¼" Mineral Fiber Board

23-Metal Border Strip

24-Crushed Stone Drainage Border

25-2" Waterproof Rigid Insulation

26-Bituminous Waterproofing

27-12" Reinforced Concrete Masonry Foundation Wall with #4 Rebars

28-Vermiculite Cavit Insulation

29-Poured, Reinforced, Continuous Concrete Footing; Set 2" Below the Frost Line

30-6 Mil Polyethylene Silt Shield

31-Graded Gravel Drainage Perforated PVC Drainage Pipe

32-R-38 & R-19 Batt Insulation; Total Roof = R-60

33-2 × 12 Rafters, 12"O.C.

34-Blocking

35-Nailer for Ceiling

36-6 Mil Polyethylene Vapor Barrier

37-⅝" Gypsum Wall Board Taped & Compounded with 3 Coats. To Be Painted

38-6" × ½" Painted Poplar Base

39-Select Oak Strip Flooring-²⁵⁄₃₂" × 2½". Sand, Stain & Finish with 3 Coats of Moisture Curing Polyurethane

40-5 Lb. Building Paper

41-¾" Plywood Subfloor

42-3 Layer Insulated Retractable Film Shades

43-Shim

44-Triple Glazed Insulating, Vinyl Clad Casement Windows, R = 3.12

45-Insect Screen

46-Painted Hardwood Sill & Trim

47-8" × 8" × ½" Black Slate Flooring

48-Cement Mortar

49-1½" Thick Reinforced Concrete Bed

50-6 Mil Polyethylene Cleavage Membrane

51-¾" Exterior Grade Plywood Subfloor

52-R-19 Batt Insulation

53-Chicken Wire Support

54-2 × 12 Header & Floor Joists

55-2 × 8 Sill

56-½" Diameter Anchor Bolt Fixed in Mortar

57-Foil Faced Insulation

58-2" Reinforced Cement Bed

59-6 Mil Polyethylene Vapor Barrier

60-Crushed Stones

61-Earth

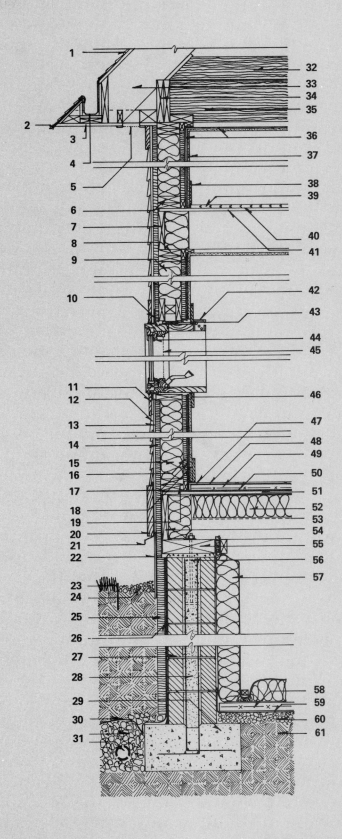

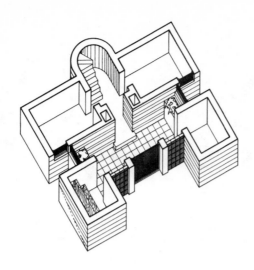

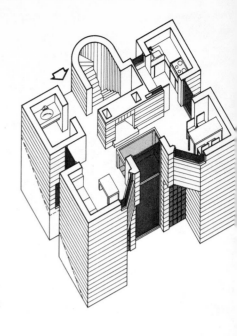

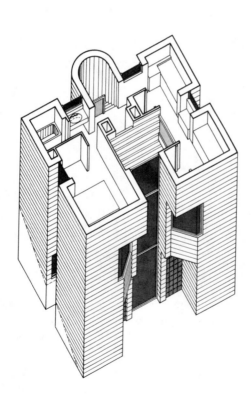

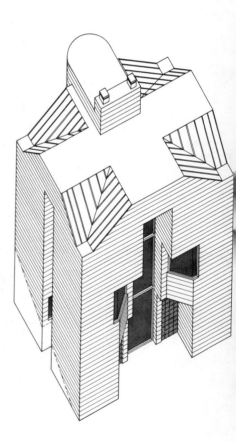

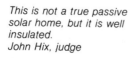

This is not a true passive solar home, but it is well insulated.
John Hix, judge

The interior space has been organized into two areas with all living areas on the south side and all service areas on the north side.
G. Nino Rico and Giancarlo Garofalo, designers

Rico and Garofalo

G. Nino Rico and
Giancarlo Garofalo

There's a formal air to this house that appeals to many.

You see it in the basement greenhouse, the two-bedroom second floor, the suggested landscaping.

The prospective builder should study the first-floor plan to determine whether it offers sufficient space. A plus is the planning of bathroom facilities on two floors.

By G. Nino Rico and Giancarlo Garofalo

This one-family, passive solar prototype house is located on a ravine in suburban Toronto, where available building lots are generally small due to the escalation of land costs. The house is built on a slope with the basement walls below grade except for the south elevation. This natural land condition, together with a row of trees on the north side, acts as a buffer zone to the winter winds.

The house has a compact design in order to minimize the exterior surface area, thus avoiding heat dispersion.

The interior space has been organized into two areas, with all living areas on the south side and all service areas on the north side.

In winter, the deciduous trees allow the sun to enter the interior space directly through the greenhouse window. The greenhouse heats up during the day, allowing the "Thermal Mass" of the ground level floor and the central wall (both built of heavy masonry) to retain heat during the day and release it at night. The fireplace and furnace chimney are also incorporated into the central wall, allowing further heat savings.

In summer, the recessed glass openings prevent direct sunlight from entering during the hottest hours of the day, thus minimizing the heat buildup. The "Thermal Mass" also retards the warming of the house until evening, while the position of the windows provides excellent ventilation.

Technical Data
Project
One-family Prototype House
Gross square feet
994
Location
Toronto, Ontario, Canada
7,000 degree days
Elevation, 525 feet

Materials
Decorated concrete block veneer exterior; decorated block and drywall interior; built-up roof and metal roof; carpet, interior rooms; hardwood floor in corridors
Type.
Compact, passive solar

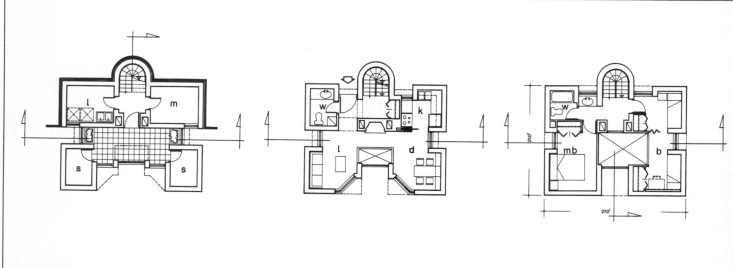

Floor Plans

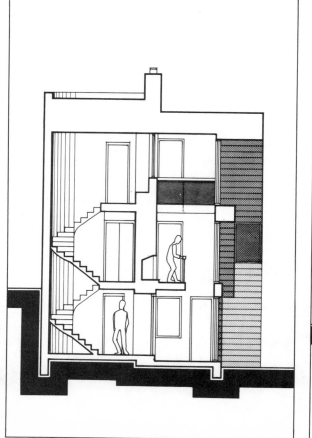

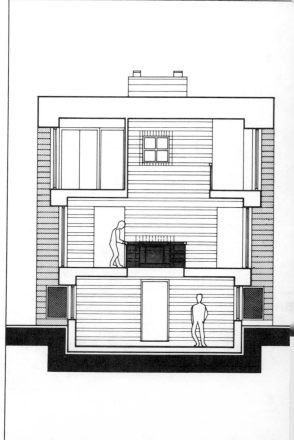

Sections

Wall Section

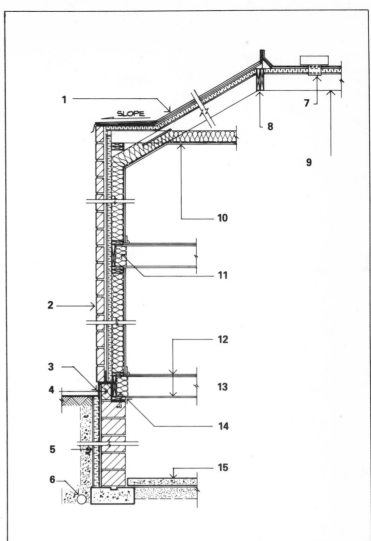

SLOPE

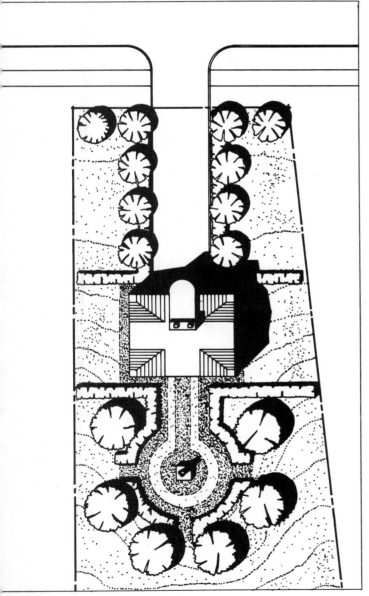

Site Plan

1-Pre-finish Metal Roof
   on Build-up Roof
   1½" Rigid Insul. (R-6)
   ⅜" Plywood
   Vapour Barrier
   2×8 Roof Rafter
2-4" Conc. Block
   Gal. Metal Block Ties @
   16" Vert. & @ 32" Horiz.
   1" Air Space
   15# Building Paper
   1½" Expand. Polystyrene
   Insul. (R-6) Sheathing
   2×6 Wood Studs @
   16"O/C with Double Top
   Plate & 2×6 Girt @
   Mid Ht.
   R-20 Batt Insulation
   Between Studs
   Vapour Barrier
   ½" Drywall & Finish
3-6 Mil Poly Flashing
   6" Behind Block
   ⅜" Ø Weep Holes @
   2'-0"O/C @ Top of
   Foundation
4-Solid Block
   Top Courses
5-2 Coats Bitumen on 2"
   Ext. Type Poly Insul. on
   ½" Cement Parging on
   12" Dec. Conc. Block
6-6" Min. Granula Fill Over
   & Around 4" Weeping
   Tiles

7-Roof Vent
8-2-2×10 W'd Beam
9-Build-up Roofing on 1½"
   Polystyrene Insul.
   ⅜" Plywood
   2×8 Roof Joist @
   16"O/C
10-2×6 Joist @ 16"O/C
   R-32 Batt Insul.
   Vapour Barrier
   ½" Drywall & Finish
11-R-20 Batt Insul.
   Vapour Barrier
   Solid Wood Blocking
   Between Joist
   4 Mil Polyethylene
12-⅜" Hardwood Floor
   ⅝" T&G Plywood
   2×10 Wood Joist @
   16"O/C
   ½" Drywall & Finish
13-6 Mil Polyethylene
   Dampproofing Course
14-2×6 Base Plate
   Anchored on Foundation
   Wall with ½" Ø Anchor
   Bolts @ 6'-8" Max.
15-4" Conc. Slab on 6 Mil
   Polyethylene 5" Granular
   Fill on Grade

143

Perspective

Strong form—good flexibility and variety.
Don Metz, judge

. . . the whole design scheme can be implemented in phases, thereby reducing the initial capital expenditure.
Arunas Rumsa, designer

Rumsa

Arunas Rumsa

This house blends comfortably with the Lake Michigan countryside. Inside, it will both surprise and please visitors because of the center diagonal wall.

The designer has presented options for those who do or do not want a basement.

By Arunas Rumsa

The building is located on a fairly level site which gently slopes down to Lake Michigan. Dunegrass and a few small evergreen and cottonwood trees are the only vegetation that exists in the sandy soil.

Lake Michigan has a tempering effect on the climate. Air conditioning is not really a necessity; a fan should be used to circulate the humid air.

The winters are not as cold as they are inland; however, lake effect precipitation results in a heavy snowfall and frequent cloud cover, making the site unattractive for solar heating.

The design is intended for people interested in a starter house or a small second home. It is appealing because the whole design scheme can be implemented in phases, thereby reducing the initial capital expenditure. A different composition of house, garage, and walks will make the house adaptable to most of the lakefront sites in the area.

Through the use of a low house profile and natural materials (wood shingles), the house is integrated into the beach environment. Cutouts in the basic rectangular form are used to address the entry and the lake.

Other features include optional basement floor plan (without compromising the design scheme) and an unfinished attic space that can be finished later to accommodate future spatial needs.

Technical Data
Project
Lake Michigan Residence
Gross square feet
1,000
Location
St. Joseph, Michigan
6,462 degree days
Elevation, 605 feet

Materials
2 × 6 wood frame, shingle exterior, drywall interior
Type
Well insulated (walls, R-28, roof, R-44)

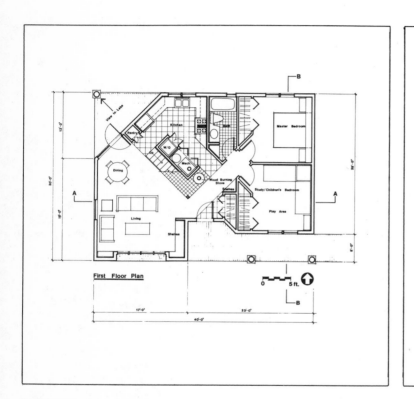

First Floor Plan

0 5 ft.

17'-0"   23'-0"

40'-0"

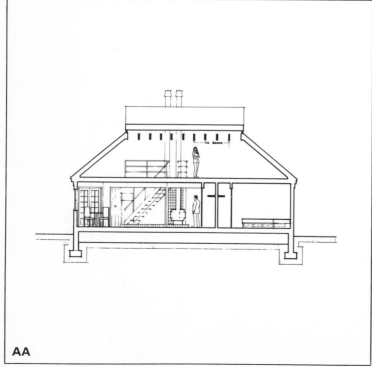

AA

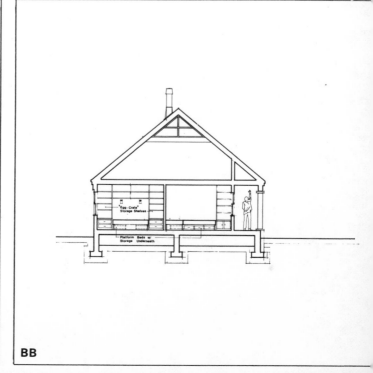

BB

Wall Section

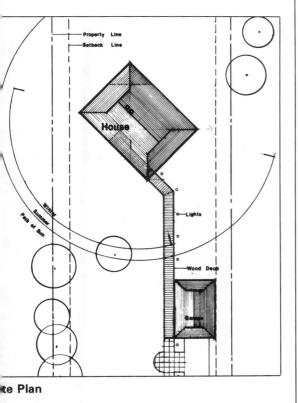

e Plan

1-Cedar Shingles (Dipped)
2-Building Paper
3-½″ Plywood Roof
   Sheathing
4-Air Space
5-2″ × 6″ Wd. Plate
6-Galy. Stl. Drip-Edge
7-1″ × 4″ Wd. Trim Over
8-1″ × 12″ Wd. Trim
9-Contin. Vent w/Insect
   Screen
10-Wd. Trim Pc.
11-(3) 2″ × 12″ w/½″
   Spacers
12-Cedar Shingles (Dipped)
13-Building Paper
14-½″ Plywd. Sheathing
15-2″ × 6″ Wd. Framing
16-2″ × 6″ Wd. Plate
17-2″ × 12″

18-Stl. Anchor Bolt
19-2″ × 12″ Treated Wd.
   Plate Over Sill Sealer
20-Backfill
21-Grade
22-Sand
23-Waterproofing
24-½″ Gypsum Board
   (Screwed to Rafters)
25-6 Mil Vapor Barrier
26-1″ Rigid Insulation
27-10″ Batt Insulation
28-¾″ Plywood Subfloor
29-2″ × 10″ Wd. Joists
30-½″ Gypsum Board
31-Double-Hung Window
   (Triple Glazed Shown)
   Caulk Around Windows

32-½″ Gypsum Board
   (Screwed to Studs)
33-6 Mil Vapor Barrier
34-1″ Rigid Insulation
35-5½″ Batt Insulation
36-Tile or Carpet over
   ¾″ Plywood Subfloor
37-5½″ Batt Insulation
38-2″ × 12″ Wd. Joists
39-Duct-Space
   12″ G.M.U. Fd'n Wall
   w/Horizontal Reinf. Bond
   Beam w/(2) #4 Rebars at
   Top Course
40-2″ Rigid Insulation
   (Optional)
41-6 Mil Vapor Barrier
42-Sand
43-2'-0″ × 1'-0″ Conc. Ftg.
   in (2) #5 Stl. Rebars. #4
   Dowel

Perspective

The area below the deck and second-story dining area expands this little house significantly. Circulation space is admirably minimal. Good zoning, views, and light all around.
Don Metz, judge

In order to save energy, the house has been kept small, well-insulated, caulked, and weatherstripped.
Homer Russell and Carol Nugent, designers

Russell and Nugent

**Homer Russell and
Carol Nugent**

Three levels, each with its own deck, three bedrooms
and other spaces for sleeping, complete privacy in the
spacious third-floor master bedroom—here's a house
that fits your needs and your dreams if your site is
near the ocean.

By Homer Russell and Carol Nugent

A slightly larger version of this house was designed
and built by the owner and his wife last summer, for
use during both summer and winter.

The couple had specific objectives, that the house be
inexpensive and easy to build, and the design be com-
patible with traditional island architecture.

The house site is 300 feet from the edge of 150-foot
bluffs overlooking the Atlantic. The view from the
ground floor is screened by a dense, eight-foot high
thicket of wild bayberry. As a result, all of the common spaces have been placed on the second floor,
with large east- and south-facing windows.

The site is quite hilly, covered in the summer with
lush vegetation, and surrounded by few other houses.
The soil contains some clay.

In order to save energy, the house has been kept
small, well-insulated, caulked, and weatherstripped.
Harsh winter temperatures are moderated somewhat
by the Gulf Stream, but severe gales are frequent,
requiring the letting in of wind bracing in addition to
the plywood sheathing. Sufficient and carefully installed flashing is essential to keep out wind-driven
rain; gutters and downspouts are useless.

There are few windows on the west and north sides.

Building materials have been selected for their thermal
efficiency, weathering capabilities, and construction
tightness.

The house is solar oriented, and a coal stove will be
supplemented by a 20,000 Btu/h kerosene mobile
home heater.

Technical Data
Project
Block Island House
Gross square feet
980
Location
Off coast of Rhode Island
5,634 degree days
Elevation, 150 feet

Materials
Wood frame, cedar shingles,
block foundation
Type
Passive solar

Site Plan

SOUTHEAST ROAD

LIGHTHOUSE

EXISTING STONE WALLS

ATLANTIC OCEAN

all Section

-6″ Foil-Faced Batt
Insul. (R-19 Min.)
-½″ GWB
Note: All Foil on Insul. to
Face Living Space
-Double Glazing
-6″ Batt Insul. (R-19 Min.)
-2 × 6 Studs 16″ O.C.
-⅝″ Oak Fin. Floor
-⅝″ Ply. Subfloor
-6″ Batt Insul. (R-19 Min.)
-2″ Rigid Insul.
-Vapor Barrier
-Frost Line 3′-6″ Below
Grade
-290# Asphalt Roofing
-15# Bldg. Paper
-½″ Ply Sheathing
-2 Layers Cedar Shingles
Under First 2 Rows of
Roofing
-Eave Vent
-8″ Lead Flash & Caulk
-10″ Alum. Pan Flash &
Caulk
-White Cedar Shingles, 5″
Exp.
-½″ Ply Sheathing
-2 × 6 P.T. Sill
-Sill Sealer
-8″ C.M.U.

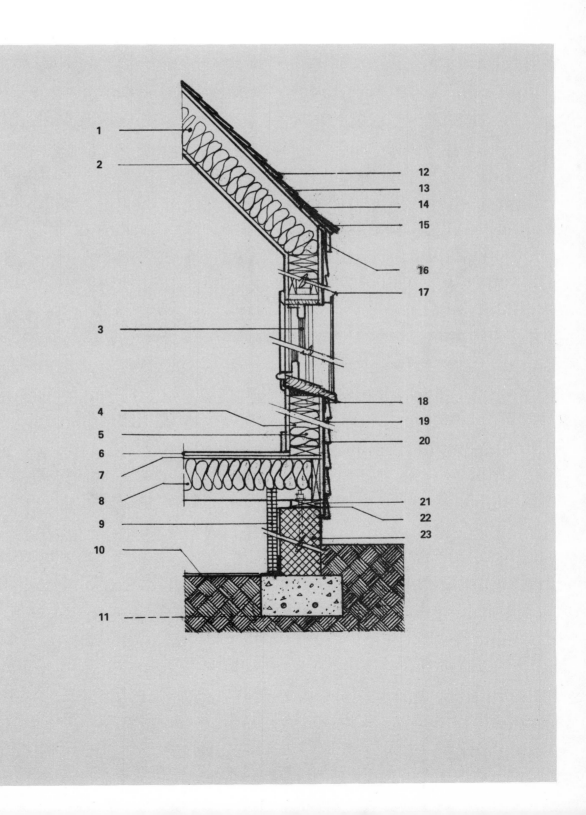

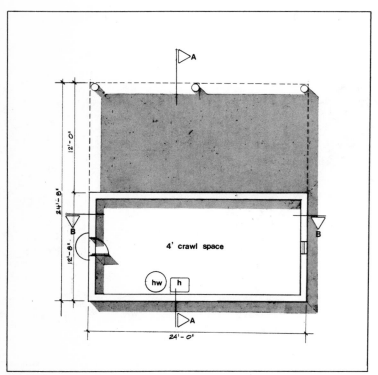

Foundation

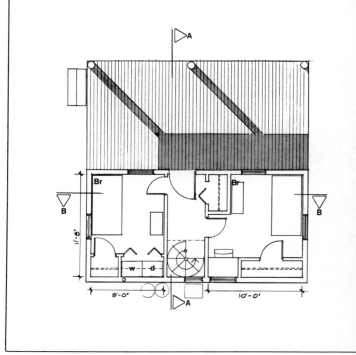

First Floor Plan

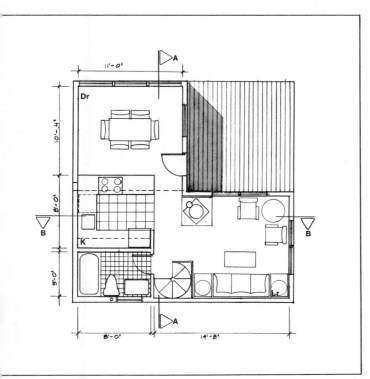

Second Floor Plan

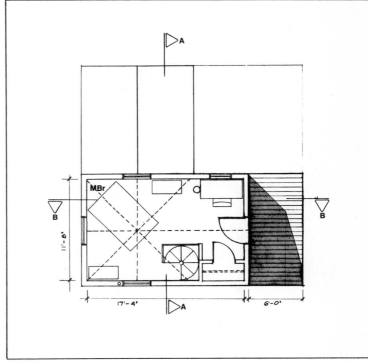

Third Floor Plan

153

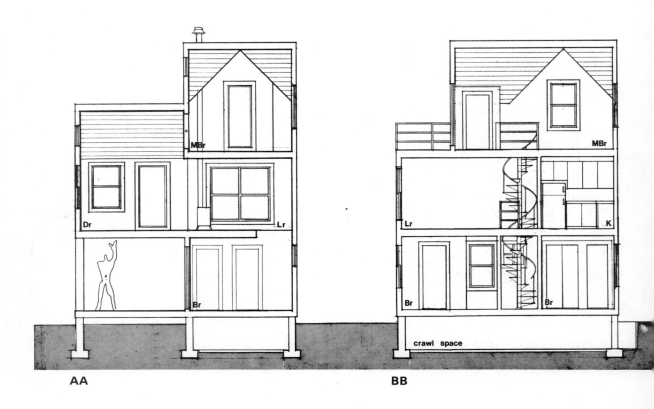

AA

BB

MBr

Dr

Lr

Br

MBr

Lr

K

Br

Br

crawl space

154

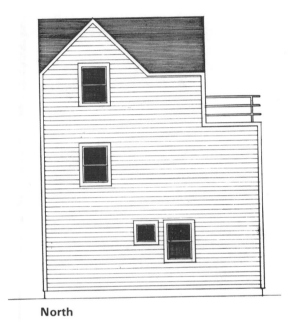

North

West

South

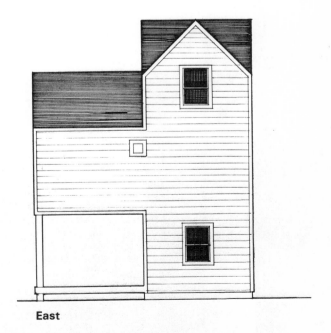

East

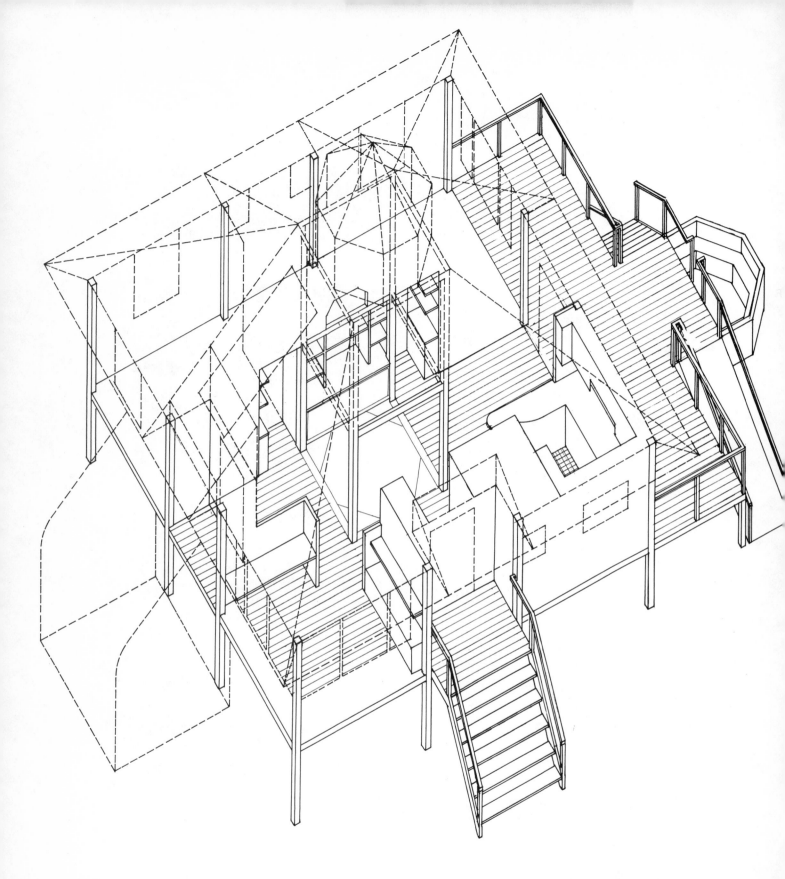

Axonometric

The formal plan is well conceived, but it is as if the designer had to think of functions to put in the rooms created by the geometry.
John Hix, judge

The entertainment space provides for typical electronic equipment of a future home.
Roberto Sotolongo, designer

Despite the formal geometry, the floor plan seems to work well, especially in three dimensions.
Don Metz, judge

Sotolongo

Roberto L. Sotolongo

The competition judges noted with approval the formality of this design, but cautioned prospective owner-builders to study carefully the floor plan to visualize whether it would be adaptable to their planned use of the house.

The belvedere, or cupola serves a dual purpose, providing ventilation as well as serving as a focal point of the design.

This is a thoughtful arrangement, well suited to a semi-tropical setting.

By Roberto L. Sotolongo

The house is designed as a prototype dwelling for the hot, humid climate of the southeastern United States. The specific site chosen is a beach lot near Charleston, South Carolina, with a climate of warm, humid summers and moderate winters.

The house, especially the public area, is oriented to provide the best views of the ocean and take advantage of prevailing breezes. A garden greenhouse on the south and deck/hot tub on the north enhance the north/south axis of the floor plan. The berm and new evergreens help protect the house from winter winds. Existing live oaks and overhangs shade the house from afternoon sun. The house is raised to protect it from coastal flooding and to improve natural ventilation.

The entertainment space provides for the typical electronic equipment of a future home. This versatile area serves as a work station during the day, entertainment focus of the evening, and guest room.

The seating area, under the octagonal belvedere, becomes a symbolic focus and increases natural ventilation.

A storage zone divides the public and private areas. The bathroom serves as a buffer during the afternoon to cool the public space. Zoning also allows the private area to be cooled or heated separately.

The bedrooms are characterized by ceiling spaces with hot air exhausts for cooling.

The optional greenhouse augments winter heating and allows vegetables and fruits to be grown year-round. A solar hot water system is used for hot water needs, and a heat pump facilitates heating and cooling demands.

Technical Data
Project
Beach House
Gross square feet
996

Location
Ten miles south of Charleston, South Carolina
2,033 degree days
Materials
Wood post-and-beam structure, tongue-and-groove wood plank floors and ceiling, exterior cedar siding

Type
Passive solar with natural ventilation

Section AA

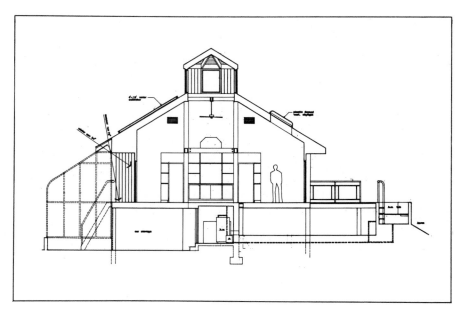

Section BB

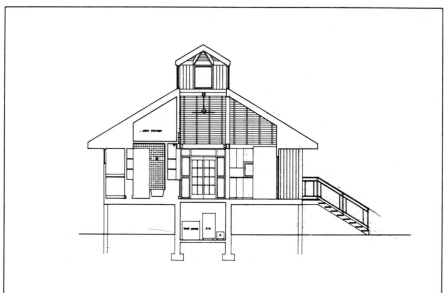

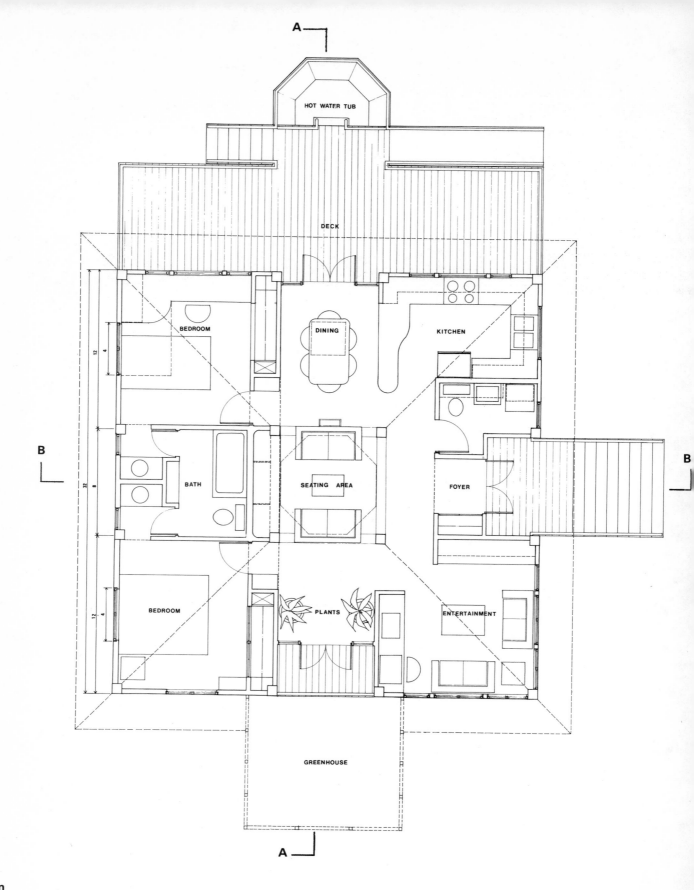

A

HOT WATER TUB

DECK

B

BEDROOM

DINING

KITCHEN

32

12

4

BATH

SEATING   AREA

FOYER

B

8

12

4

BEDROOM

PLANTS

ENTERTAINMENT

A

GREENHOUSE

A

Floor Plan

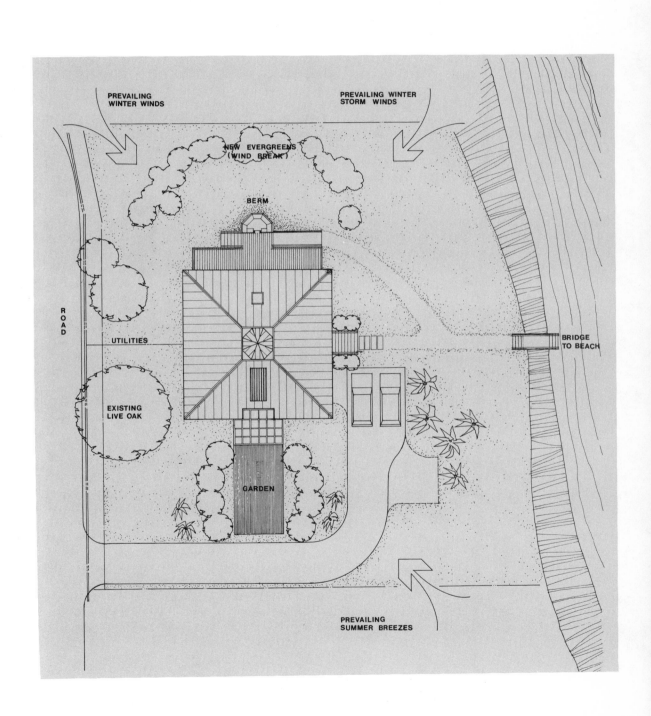

Perspective

A rational and practical plan
with an eclectic disposition.
I like the combination.
Don Metz, judge

Positive house ventilation is
accomplished with a large
fan located at the ridge of
the trombe wall.
Brian G. Swier, designer

162

Swier and Costantin

**Brian G. Swier and
Michael Costantin**

Yin or Yang is a house that promises comfort in a
small space. Some of its features—the loft, for example—lift it out of the ranks of dull small homes.

By Brian G. Swier

Yin or Yang is a proposal for a prototypical, two-bedroom house that can be situated on a quarter-acre or
larger lot.

The square plan interlocks two opposing structural
systems: the south-facing masonry trombe wall and
the remaining superinsulated wood-frame wall.

A central wood-burning stove is the primary heat
source whenever solar energy is insufficient. A heat
pump is provided for supplemental heating during the
winter and cooling during the summer. The shaded
trombe wall also helps absorb excess heat, especially
when vented with earth-cooled drafts from the crawl
space. Positive house ventilation is accomplished with
a large fan located at the ridge of the trombe wall.

The dialectic between concrete masonry and wood
framing is expressed on the exterior, and allows the
house to be interpreted alternately as a humble ranch-
style home or as a pseudo-classical villa. These di-
verse scales also exist on the interior as the ambiguity
between the "bigness" of the space and windows and
the "smallness" of doors and trim articulations.

Technical Data
Project
Yin or Yang
Gross square feet
1,000
Location
Philadelphia
5,144 degree days

Materials
Concrete masonry,
wood frame

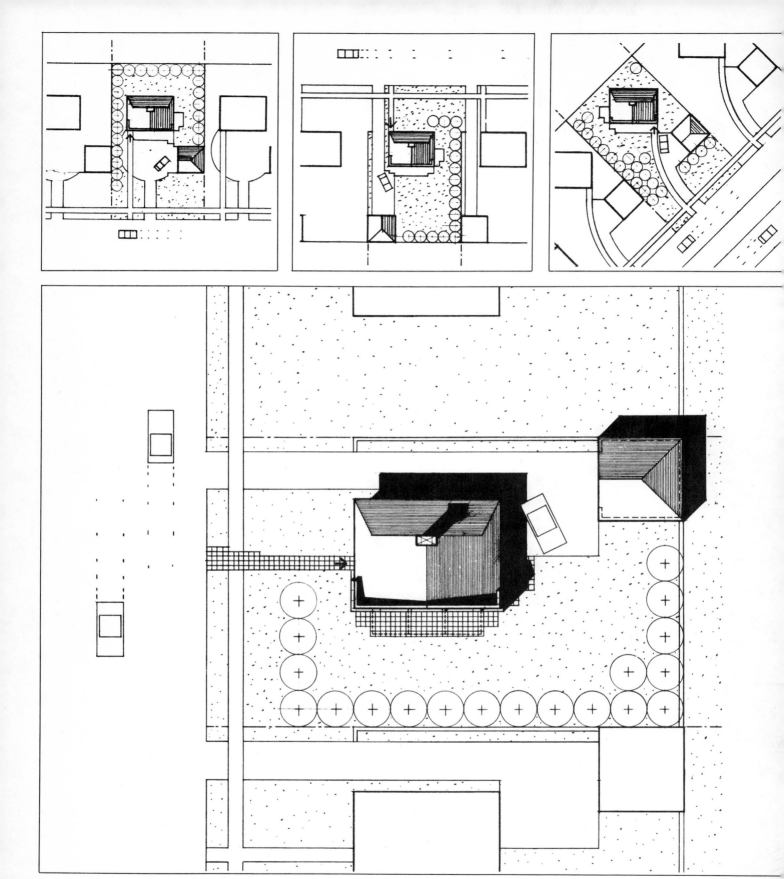

Site Plans

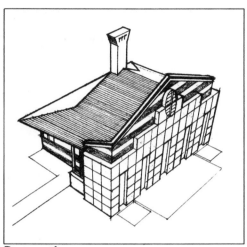

Perspective

Perspective

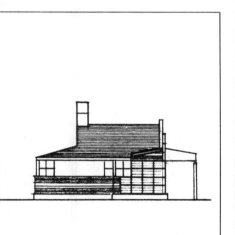

West

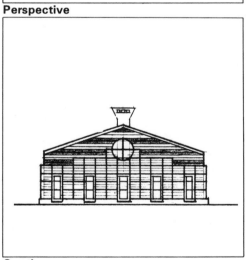

South

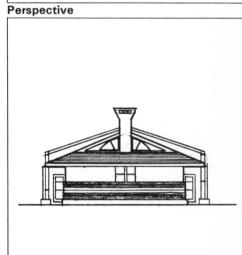

North

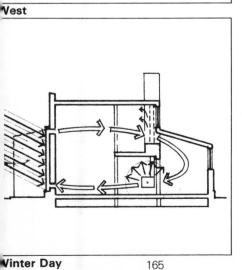

Winter Day

165

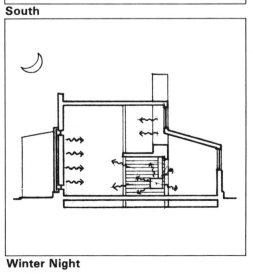

Winter Night

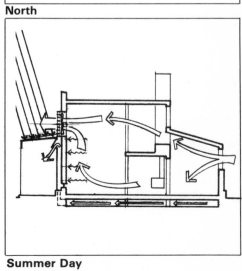

Summer Day

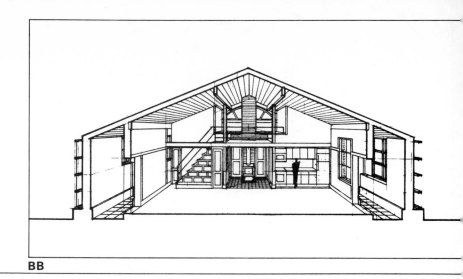

BB

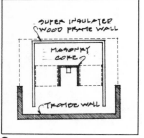

Concept

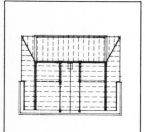

Structure

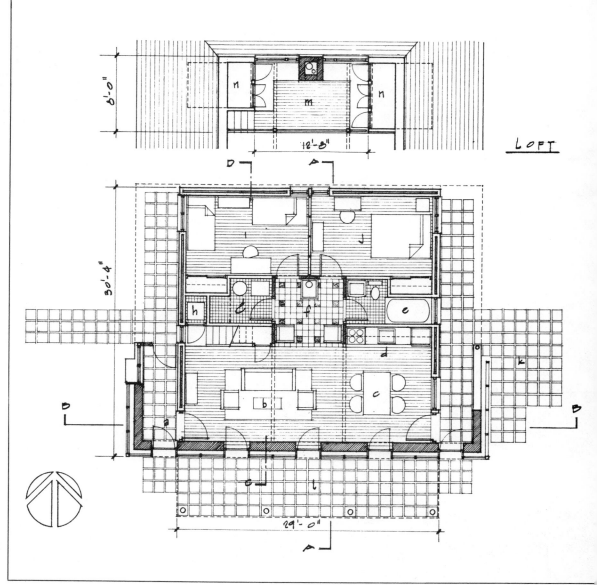

LOFT

Floor Plan

Legend

a. Entry
b. Living
c. Dining
d. Kitchen
e. Bath
f. Hearth
g. Mechanical

h. Laundry
i. Bedroom
j. Bedroom
k. Patio
l. Porch
m. Loft
n. Storage

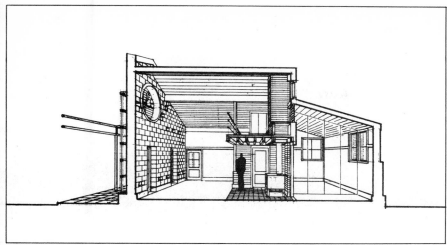

AA

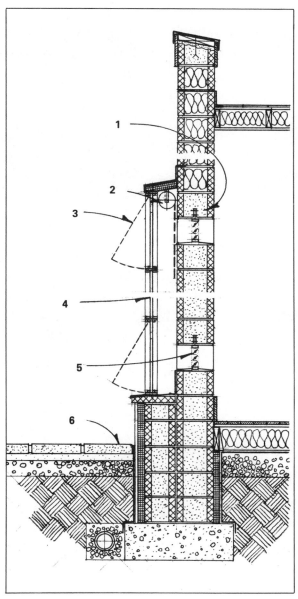

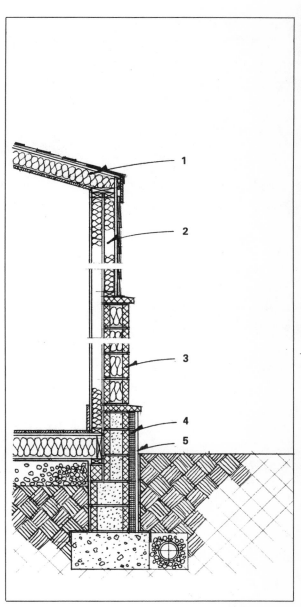

Wall Sections

1-Cement Filled Concrete Block
2-Retractable Thermal Shade
3-Operable Thermal Vent
4-Thermal Glass
5-Operable Louvers
6-Concrete Pavers

1-2 × 6 Roof Rafters @ 16" O.C.
2-Double 2 × 3 Staggered Stud Wall @ 2' O.C.
3-Batt Insulation Filled Concrete Blocks
4-Rigid Insulation
5-Lath & Cement

167

Perspective

An economical scheme
which adapts well to prefab
components and tract house
economies. Easily expand-
able to three or four
bedrooms.
Don Metz, judge

The house can be built in
twenty three working days.
*George Hugh Tsuruoka,
architect*

Tsuruoka

George Hugh Tsuruoka

This house is relatively inexpensive, and quick to build (twenty-three days). It can be expanded, too, if the need for a larger home arises.

The 12/12 roof pitch minimizes snow loading, reducing roof framing, and creates a feeling of bigness in a rather small house. The house contains a solar attic (18 percent heating contribution), direct gain through the south-facing glass (7-9 percent solar gain), a Plen-Wood ductless heating system that saves up to 35 percent of the heating costs; and the house is thermally efficient, requiring only 5.2 Btu/DD/ft².

By George Hugh Tsuruoka

This house has been designed for a new community of affordable homes in the upper Midwest. The land, a former farm, is flat, without special views, and without any significant micro-climate.

The 12/12 roof pitch minimizes snow loading, reducing roof framing, and creates a feeling of bigness in a rather small house. The house contains a solar attic (18 percent heating contribution), direct gain through the south-facing glass (7-9 percent solar gain), a Plen-Wood ductless heating system that saves up to 35 percent of the heating costs; and the house is thermally efficient, requiring only 5.2 Btu/DD/ft².

The house has been designed to be componentized, and delivered to the site on one flatbed truck.

The design consists of four small boxes that can be built with minimum effort, are easy to frame, and economical to build. All framing is on twenty-four-inch centers and has minimum waste.

The living room, kitchen, and family/dining room have sloping ceilings and are open to one another, creating an additional feeling of space.

The main outdoor living area also serves as an entrance court. Added privacy can be achieved by erecting a fence on the east side of the deck. A second outdoor living area opens off the living room.

The house can be faced and sited on small lots in many different ways, and the garage can be placed in several different locations to form the private entrance court.

Technical Data
Project
Solar Attic House
Gross square feet
998
Location
Upper Midwest
6,200 degree days
Elevation, 400 feet

Materials
Wood
Type
Solar attic, Plen-Wood heating system, superinsulated

Floor Plan

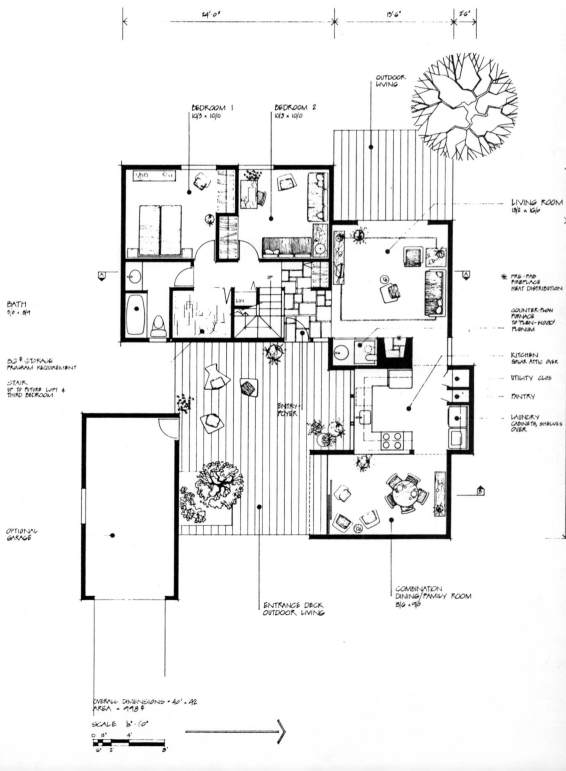

24'-0"   15'6"   2'6"

OUTDOOR LIVING

BEDROOM 1
10/3 × 10/0

BEDROOM 2
10/3 × 10/0

LIVING ROOM
13/2 × 16/0

✳ PRE-FAB FIREPLACE HEAT DISTRIBUTION

COUNTER-FLOW FURNACE TO 'FILM-WOOD' PLENUM

KITCHEN
SOLAR ATTIC OVER

UTILITY CLOS

PANTRY

LAUNDRY
CABINETS, SHELVES OVER

BATH
5/0 × 8/9

85 ℉ STORAGE
PROGRAM REQUIREMENT

STAIR
UP TO FUTURE LOFT &
THIRD BEDROOM

UP

LIN

A

ENTRY-FOYER

OPTIONAL GARAGE

ENTRANCE DECK
OUTDOOR LIVING

COMBINATION
DINING/FAMILY ROOM
13/6 × 9/6

OVERALL DIMENSIONS = 40' × 42'
AREA = 998 ℉

SCALE ⅛" = 1'-0"

0 1' 4'
6' 2' 8'

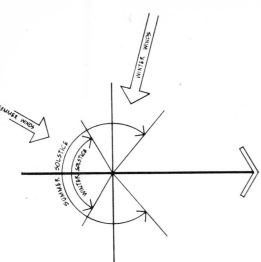

Site Plan

Section AA

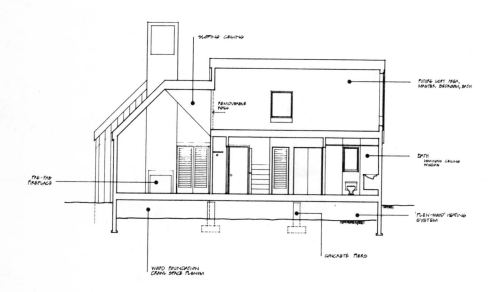

SLOPING CEILING

FUTURE LOFT AREA,
MASTER BEDROOM, BATH

REMOVABLE
WALL

BATH
LUMINOUS CEILING
WINDOW

PRE-FAB
FIREPLACE

'PLEN-WOOD' HEATING
SYSTEM

CONCRETE PIERS

WOOD FOUNDATION
CRAWL SPACE PLENUM

Section BB

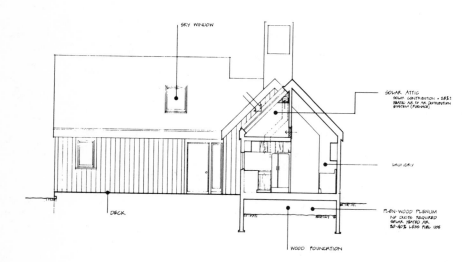

SKY WINDOW

SOLAR ATTIC
SOLAR CONTRIBUTION + 28%
HEATED AIR TO AIR DISTRIBUTION
SYSTEM (FURNACE)

LAUNDRY

DECK

PLEN-WOOD PLENUM
NO DUCTS REQUIRED
SOLAR HEATED AIR
30-40% LESS FUEL USE

WOOD FOUNDATION

Wall Section

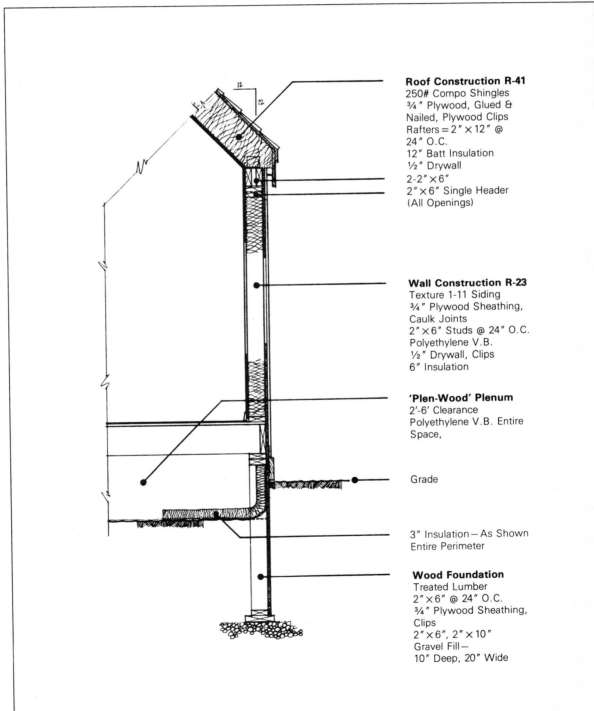

Roof Construction R-41
250# Compo Shingles
¾″ Plywood, Glued &
Nailed, Plywood Clips
Rafters = 2″ × 12″ @
24″ O.C.
12″ Batt Insulation
½″ Drywall
2-2″ × 6″
2″ × 6″ Single Header
(All Openings)

Wall Construction R-23
Texture 1-11 Siding
¾″ Plywood Sheathing,
Caulk Joints
2″ × 6″ Studs @ 24″ O.C.
Polyethylene V.B.
½″ Drywall, Clips
6″ Insulation

'Plen-Wood' Plenum
2'-6' Clearance
Polyethylene V.B. Entire
Space,

Grade

3″ Insulation — As Shown
Entire Perimeter

Wood Foundation
Treated Lumber
2″ × 6″ @ 24″ O.C.
¾″ Plywood Sheathing,
Clips
2″ × 6″, 2″ × 10″
Gravel Fill —
10″ Deep, 20″ Wide

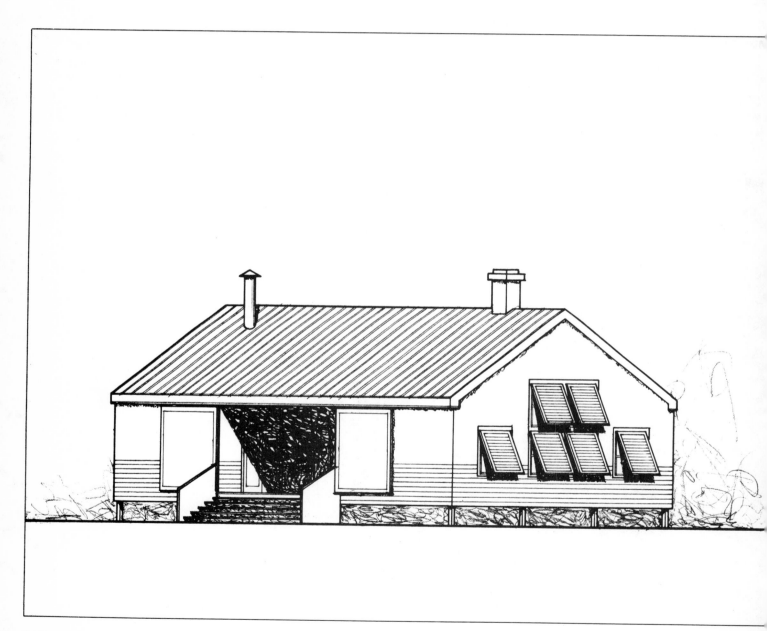

Perspective

I'd like to live in that house. It's so classic.
John Hix, judge

Large sliding doors at both ends of a central breezeway and swing-up shutters over the windows can be manipulated to secure the house when vacant, open the house to sunlight but not wind on cool days, and maximize breezes through the house on hot, humid days.
Michael Underhill, architect

Underhill

Michael Underhill

Introducing—the Texas dog-trot design, a new concept and name to most of us, but familiar to generations of Texans.

The dog-trot in this house is a 16'8" open breezeway running north and south and separating living and sleeping quarters. By opening and shutting the doors at either end, temperatures in the house can be controlled to a surprising extent.

The term dates back to the cowboy days when dogs found the open space to their liking as they chased each other in and out through the open doors.

By Michael Underhill

In a small second house for a remote site in a rural area near Houston, the traditional Texas dog-trot configuration is adapted to eliminate the need for air conditioning. Large sliding doors at both ends of a central breezeway and swing-up shutters over the windows can be manipulated to secure the house when vacant, open the house to sunlight but not to wind on cool days, and maximize breezes through the house on hot, humid days.

Technical Data
Project
Parker House
Gross square feet
982, with a breezeway
of 522 sq. ft.
Location
Near Houston, Texas
1,316 degree days
Materials
Wood

Type
Well insulated, natural
ventilation, wood frame
construction

Floor Plan

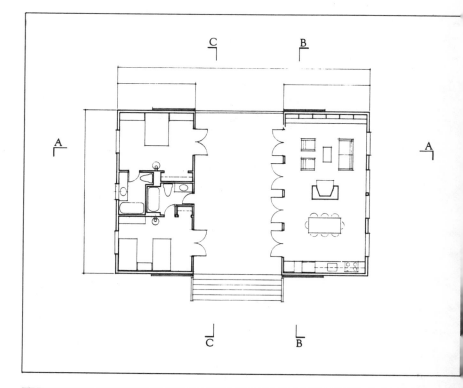

Site Plan

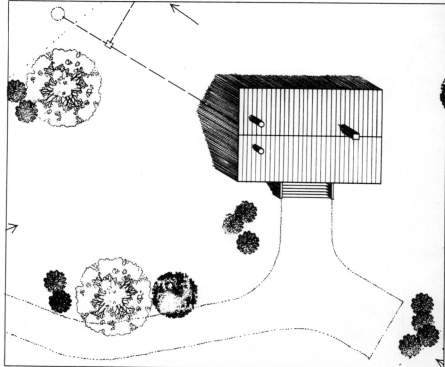

With the northern doors closed and the windows and doors closed, the winter winds are not pulled through the house. The shutters and southern sliding doors can be opened to allow sunlight into the house and breezeway.

With the southern sliding doors partially open and the northern doors open, summer breezes are channeled through the breezeway, pulling air through the open windows and doors of the two interior areas.

1- ½" Gypsum Board
2- Vapor Barrier
3- 8" Batts Insulation Between 2 × 10 Rafters 16" on Center
4- Standard Wood Hopper Window Units
5- ½" Gypsum Board
6- Vapor Barrier
7- 5" Batts Insulation
8- 2 × 6 Studs 16" on Center
9- Wood Flooring
10- Building Paper
11- ¾" Plywood Deck
12- 2 × 6 Joists 16" on Center
13- Asphalt Shingles or Standing Seam Metal
14- Roofing Felts
15- ½" Plywood Deck
16- 2 × 10 Rafters 16" on Center
17- Metal Drip Edge
18- 1 × 8 Wood Fascia
19- Sliding Door Tract
20- Wood Shingles
21- Foil Faced Building Paper
22- ½" Plywood Sheathing
23- Metal Drip Cap
24- 1¼ × 4" Wood Casing
25- Swinging Wood Shutter
26- Shiplap Wood Siding
27- Foil Faced Building Paper
28- ½" Plywood Sheathing
29- Double 2 × 10 Header
30- 2 × 4 Ribbon
31- 6 × 6 Treated Piles
32- Concrete Foundation Pads (not shown)

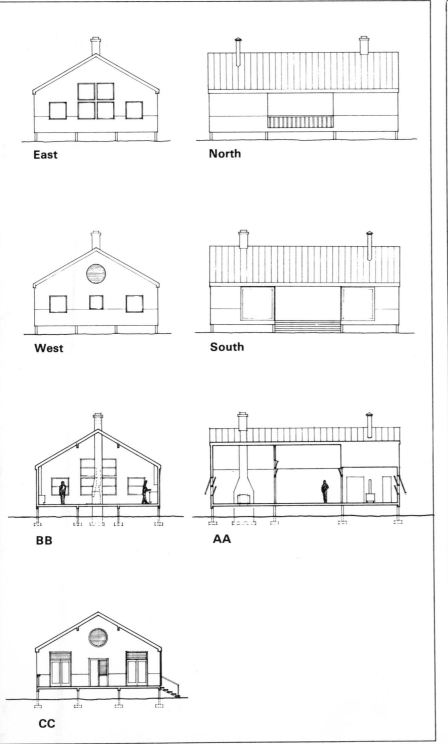

East

North

West

South

BB

AA

CC

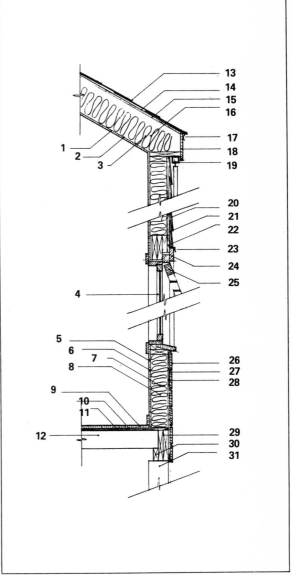

Wall Section

Sections

Perspective

Very simple, economic,
and elegant.
Don Watson, judge

Partial berming of the
houses aids the heating and
changes the scale as each
house marries with the site,
giving each a lower profile
on the horizon.
James M. Wehler, architect

Wehler

James M. Wehler

This condominium is one of a group of nine units in Terrazas Del Sol, 7,000 feet above sea level in northern New Mexico. Some noteworthy features: partial berming, solar heating, heavy insulation, and architecture that fits its Southwest setting. Competition judge Don Watson's comment summed up the beauty of this entry: "Very simple, economic, and elegant."

By James M. Wehler

The concept of Terrazas Del Sol was to offer the freedom of condominium living and the benefits of single-family residence country life, all in a compact, reasonably priced, energy-efficient package.

The project was designed to accentuate the "wide open spaces" of the Southwest while maintaining moderate high density for land efficiency. The condominium concept retains control over any possible future unsightliness through the rule of the homeowners' association, and assures future maintenance, thus guaranteeing values.

Cluster grouping of the units was chosen in order to increase density without having it become offensive. Individual security is enhanced with neighbors living close together, but terraces are carefully arranged to provide privacy.

The cluster takes on a "hacienda" or estate appearance, a style indigenous to the Southwest.

Partial berming of the houses aids the heating and changes the scale as each house marries with the site, giving each a lower profile on the horizon. Landscaped berms were constructed to modulate an otherwise flat terrain, to control drainage, to define space, and give a sense of privacy and "place."

The concept of Terrazas Del Sol is to provide for its owners the amenities of a planned unit development in a rural setting where open space, beautiful views, clean air, and efficient solar construction make for a desirable lifestyle.

Technical Data
Project
Terrazas Del Sol
Gross square feet
960 per unit
Location
Northern New Mexico
7,000 degree days
Elevation, 7,000 feet

Materials
2 x 6 wood frame, exterior stucco, interior plaster, wood cellulose insulation, built-up roof and gravel, concrete slab with Mexican tile in living areas, carpet in bedroom and bath

Type
Passive and air-active solar with electric baseboard back-up; rock storage under slab perimeter; partial earth berm; insulation of R-22 walls, R-40 roof; heat-circulating fireplace; forty-gallon solar preheat tank, with electric booster domestic water heat system

Floor Plan

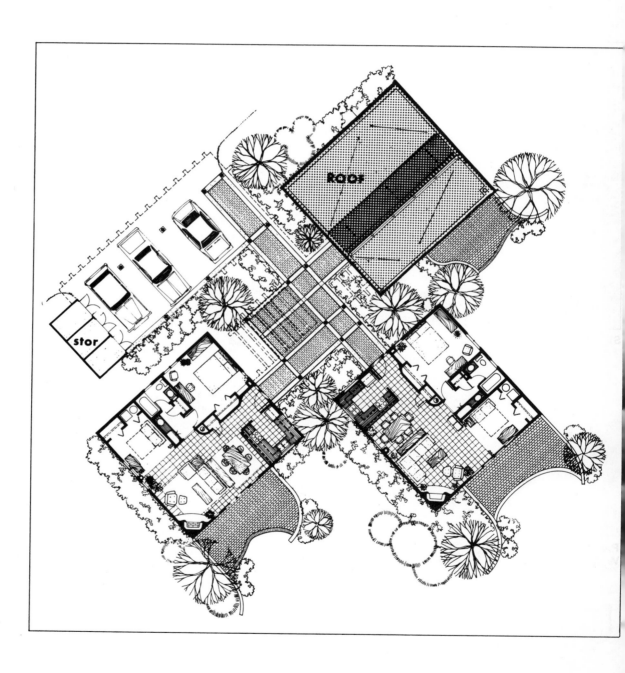

roof

stor

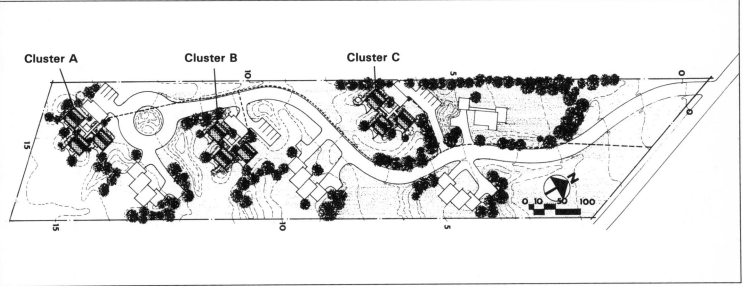

Cluster A   Cluster B   Cluster C

Site Plan

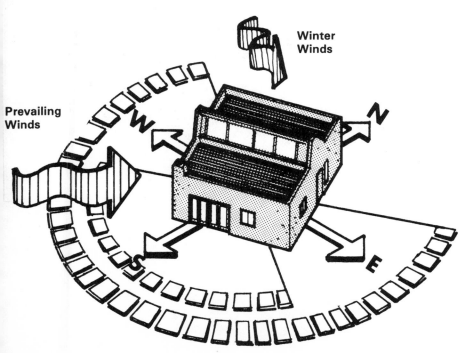

Winter
Winds

Prevailing
Winds

Section AA

Section BB

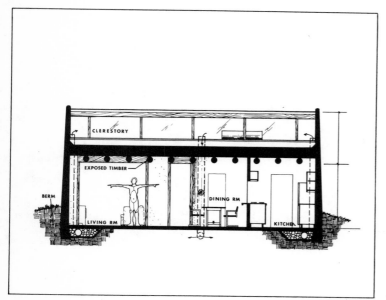

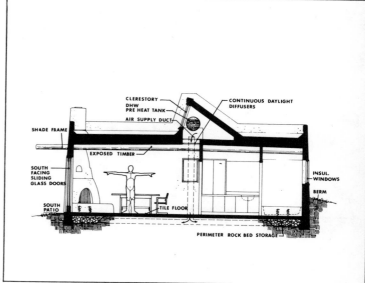

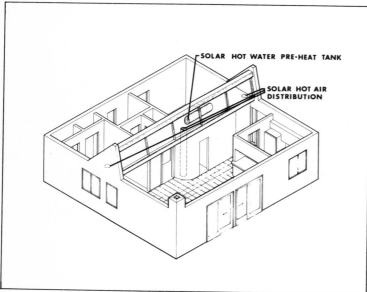

Isometric

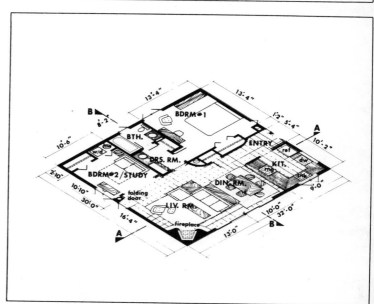

Floor Plan

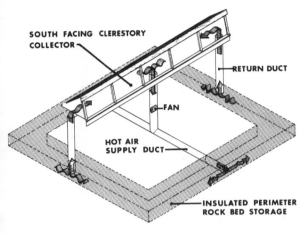

SOUTH FACING CLERESTORY
COLLECTOR

RETURN DUCT

FAN

HOT AIR
SUPPLY DUCT

INSULATED PERIMETER
ROCK BED STORAGE

Isometric

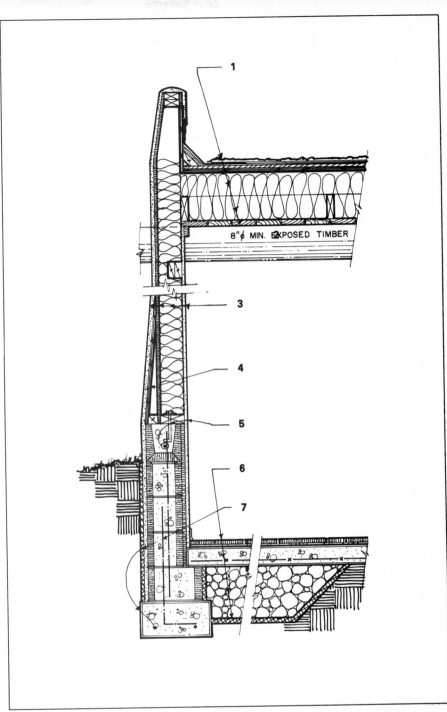

8"∅ MIN. EXPOSED TIMBER

1

2

3

4

5

6

7

1-Built-up Roof & Gravel,
4-ply on ½" Fibre Bd.
Base on ½" CDX
Plywood Deck on 2 × 6
Rafters @ 2'-0"O.C. on
2 × 6 Blocking @ 6'-0"O.C.
w/R-40 Cellulose Fibre
Insulation & 1 × 6 T&G
Aspen Ceiling Deck
2-8" ∅ Min. Exposed Timber
3-½" Gyp. Board on 2 × 6
@ 16"O.C. Wd. Frame
w/R-19 Cellulose Fibre
Insul. & ½" Fibre Bd.
Sheathing w/¾" Cement
Stucco over Galv. Stucco
Wire, Sand Float Finish

4-½" CDX Plywd. Batter-
Bd. w/2× Blk.
5-8" CMU Bd. Bm. w/1-#4
Cont., Faced w/½" Fibre
Bd. & ½" Gyp. Bd.
w/½" ∅ A.B. @
4'-0"O.C.
6-12" × 12" Conc. Tiles in
Thinset on 4" Conc. Slab
w/6" × 6" 10/10 WWF on
Rock Bd. Perimeter w/1"
Rigid Insul. Lining
7-8" CMU Filled Stem w/
1-#4 @ 4'-0" Vert. on
One Course 12" CMU on
8" × 16" Conc. Ftng.
w/2-#4 Contin. & 1" Rigid
Insul.

183

Perspective

This is a fun design.
Barry Berkus, judge

*. . . like a piece of friendly
Victoriana that actually works
very efficiently.*
Don Metz, judge

*Under the solar staircase we
find a secluded window seat
(doubles as a sleeping nook
for a guest) and below that a
"children's cave" with its
own window.*
Michael Wisniewski, architect

Wisniewski

Michael Wisniewski

Barry Berkus, one of the competition judges, said, after studying the Solar Staircase House, "This is a fun design."

Look it over and you may agree. The child's cave is certainly "fun," and a place for a child to hide his treasures.

There's something lighthearted, too, about the staircase with its window nook.

Equally important, there's a hard practicality to this house, in the allocation of space as well as its provisions for energy conservation.

By Michael Wisniewski

The Solar Staircase House addresses several issues often ignored in the rush for efficient plans and low heating bills. Siting is very flexible, and the solar staircase/hearth is a unique way of providing environmental comfort and several useful small spaces which make the compact house enjoyable to live in.

Siting
The corner porch entry along with a careful sequence of landscaping allows the house to be sited with any combination of site access/solar orientation while offering a warm and inviting entry and maintaining privacy for outdoor living/working areas.

Environmental
The staircase is slightly inflated to serve as a solar collector/storage unit filtering light into the living areas and offering a window seat in the sun.

This solves the compact house dilemma of not having enough square feet for a usable sunplace, but not wanting a direct gain situation where the living areas are hot, stuffy, and full of glare.

Social
The house is very open, but care was taken in the planning to respect the needs for privacy, and to provide a place for children. Bedrooms are cozy, private, and large enough for a study. Under the solar staircase we find a secluded window seat (doubles as a sleeping nook for a guest) and below that a "children's cave" with its own window. Above the bath is an area for a future crow's nest playroom.

Technical Data
Project
Solar Staircase House
Gross square feet
988
Location
Vermont
8,200 degree days

Materials
Wood frame, concrete frost wall, clapboard shingles or galvanized metal roof, wood windows, gypsum board, carpet, wood floor, quarry tile hearth, R-9 thermal curtains, eutectic storage tubes
Type
Highly insulated modified direct gain

1-Loft (Unfinished)
2-Window Nook
3-Child Cave
4-Phase Change Storage
5-Thermal Curtain
6-Air Duct
7-Canvas Awning-Optional

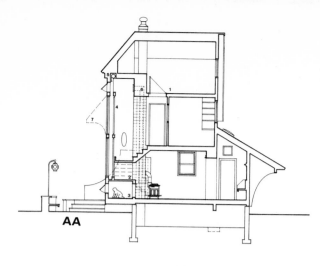

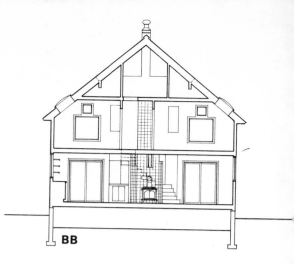

AA

BB

1-MBR
2-BR
3-Bath w/Obscure Glass
4-Loft (Unfinished) Ladder
5-Porch Skylight

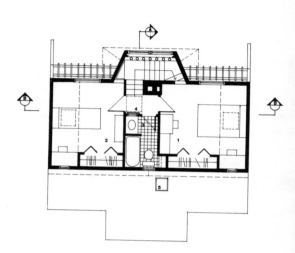

1-Corner Porch
2-Wood Storage
3-Entry w/Bench
4-Living
5-Hearth
6-Country Kitchen
7-Utility (Tankless H$_2$O Heater)
8-Window Seat/Child Cave
9-Solar Staircase
10-Air Duct
11-Trellis
12-Deck
13-Garden

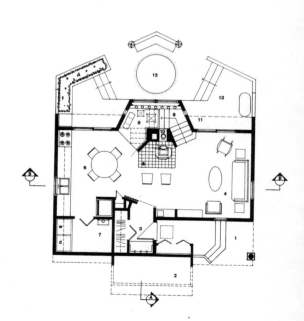

186

Site Plan Alternates

1-½" Sheathing
2-2 × 3 Strapping Nailed into Roof Rafters for Vent Space
3-2 × 12 Rafters— 2'-0"O.C.
4-12" Fiberglass Batt
5-1.2" R-7 Insulating Sheathing
6-Painted Exterior "Porch" Grade Beaded T&G Spruce
7-Shingles
8-Gal. Metal Drip Edge
9-Soffit Vent w. Insect Screen
10-2 × 10 Joists 16"O.C. Spanning North South-Bridging at Midspan

11-2 × 6 Stud Wall 2'-0"O.C. Balloon Frame East and West Walls, Platform Frame North-South Walls
12-6" Fiberglass Batt
13-1.2" R-7 Insulating Sheathing
14-Wood Clapboard 4" to Weather
15-9" Fiberglass Batt
16-2 × 10 Joists 16"O.C. Spanning North/South. Provide Bridging at Mid-span. Double Rim Joist, ¾" T&G Plywood Subfloor Nailed & Glued
17-Pressure Treated 2 × 6 w/Sill Seal

18-2" Rigid Polystyrene perimeter Insulation 2'-0" Below Exterior Grade
19-Crawl Space
20-Grade
21-Concrete or Concrete Block Frost Wall-2 Coats of Asphalt Bituminous Waterproofing on Below Grade Exterior
22-6 Mil Polyethylene Vapor Barrier
23-4" PVC Drain Tile

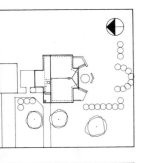
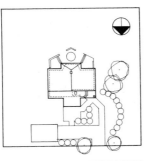
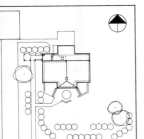
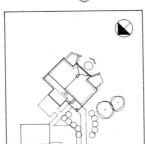

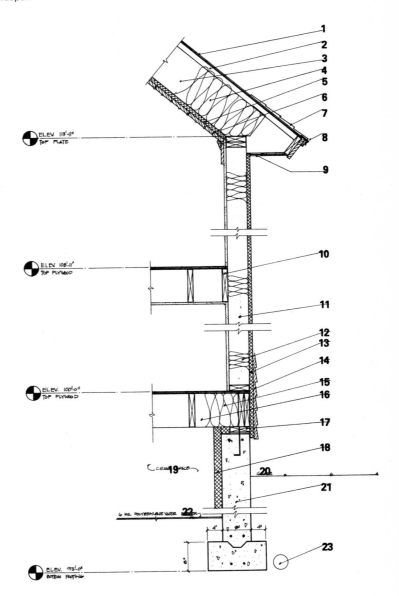

Wall Section

187

Perspective

Screwy—but cute.
Barry Berkus, judge

Good visual appeal.
Don Metz, judge

Advantages of the design
include . . . possibility of
enclosing the front entry
porch at a later date, thus
forming an entry vestibule
. . . a loft which can serve
as a TV room, study, or
future third bedroom.
Thomas Woodman, designer

Woodman

Thomas Woodman

Lots of storage space . . . an open first floor . . . bathroom facilities on two floors . . . an abundance of south-facing windows. These are some of the practical pluses of this design.

Add to those an unusual feature—a third-floor loft for meditating, TV watching, or sleeping—and the design becomes one with appeal for the many who want good planning, plus something a little different.

Judge Barry Berkus praised this design as, "Screwy—but cute."

We agree.

By Thomas Woodman

The site is in a heavily wooded residential development outside the metropolitan area of Cleveland, Ohio. The house is oriented to take advantage of the view to an existing ravine and stream which flows into a river west of the site. Because the site is heavily wooded and because we wanted to disturb the natural setting as little as possible, we based the design (especially the construction methods) on regional standards. To develop a passive or active solar design would have destroyed the natural setting.

Advantages of the design include: a living hall with flexible seating arrangements; possibility of enclosing the front entry porch at a later date, thus forming an entry vestibule; extra storage areas in crawl space and in vented space above second bedroom; a loft which can serve as a TV room, study, or future third bedroom; and a wood stove which can provide back-up heat or be the main heating source, depending on the ambitions of the tenant.

The archetypal form of the structure is so strong that using other siding methods, whether more or less expensive, or other window locations will not destroy the (farmhouse/lean-to/colonial) image that the house portrays.

Technical Data
Project
Compact House
Gross square feet
1,000
Location
Bainbridge, Ohio
6,000 degree days
Elevation, 1,050 feet

Materials
Wood siding, fiberglass shingles, concrete block, insulated glass windows
Type
Heavily insulated, standard frame construction

Site Plan

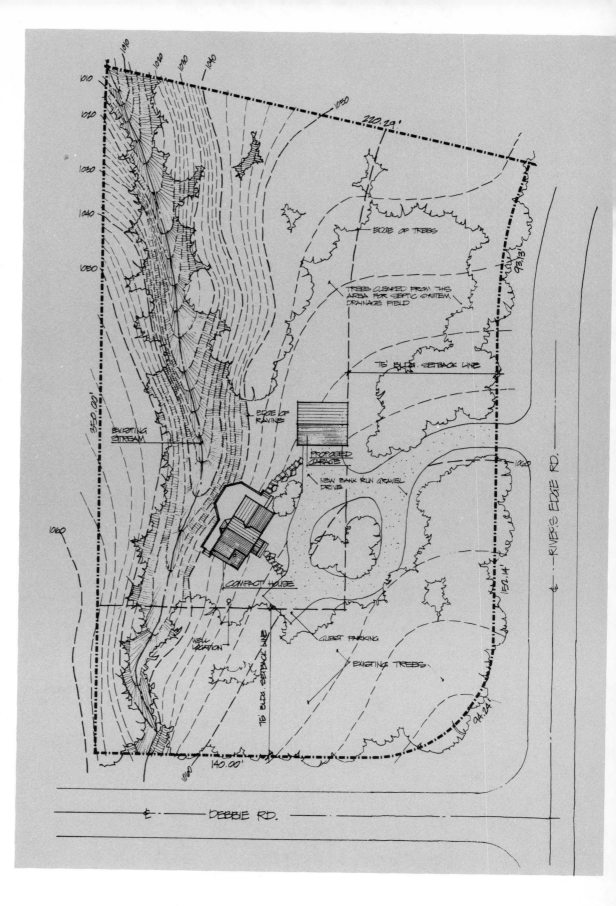

Second Floor Plan

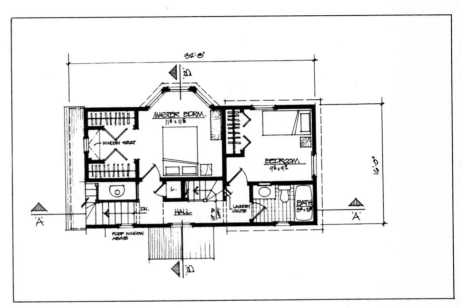

First Floor Plan

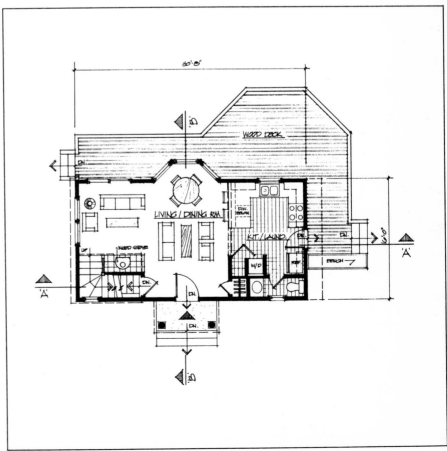

191

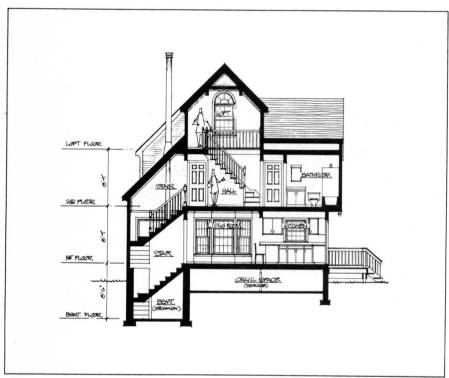

Section AA

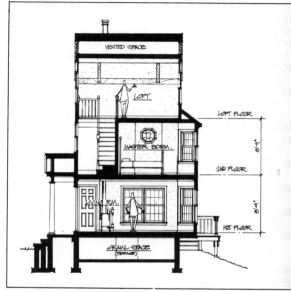

Section BB

Wall Section

1-(2)- 2×10 w/ ⅜″×9″ Stl. Plate Flitch Beam Cased Out w/ 1″× Hewn Boards

2-Hewn Boxed Wood Beams Beyond

3-1″×8″ Hewn Wd. Trim Board

4-1¼″ Clear

5-Wood Base

6-R-19 Insul.

7-2″×8″ Wd. Joists @ 16″ O.C.

8-(2)- 2×10 w/ ⅜×9″ Stl. Plate Flitch Beam Cased w/ ½″ Gypsum Board

9-R-19 Batt Insul.

10-Wood Crown

11-Wood Stool

12-Wood Casing

13-Wood Base

14-R-19 Batt Insulation

15-6″×9″ Wood Sill Plate

16-½″ Asphalt Impregnated Leveling Pad

17-½″∅×18″ Long Anchor Bolt (8′-0″ O.C. Min. 2 Per Plate)

18-½″ Expansion Material

19-2″×12″ Wood Ridge Board

20-2″×6″ Clo Joists @ 16″ O.C.

21-1″×3″ Wood Shingle Mold

22-1″×8″ Wood Fascia Board

23-½″ Plywood Soffit w/ Cont. Screened Prefinished Alum. Vent.

24-Wood Crown Mold

25-1″×10″ Wood Frieze Board

26-Prefinished Alum. Flash-Vent

27-2″×4″ Wood Ledger

28-1″×8″ Wood Fascia Board

29-Prefinished Alum. Gutter

30-½″ Plywood Soffit w/ Cont. Screened Prefinished Alum. Vent.

31-Wood Crown Mold

32-1″×10″ Wood Frieze Board

33-Clad-Double-Hung Windows w/ Insul. Glass & Screens

34-1″×6″ Wd. Trim Typ. @ All Windows Doors & Corners

35-Wood Water Table

36-1″×12″ Wood Trim Board

37-Gravel Fill Carried To Within 1″-0″ of Finished Grade

38-4″ Drain Tile

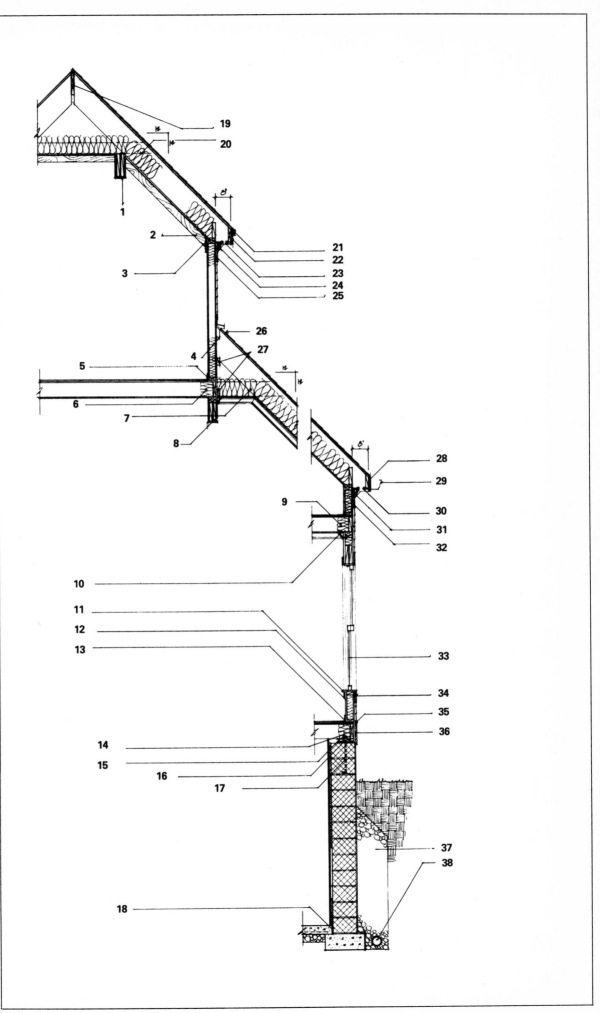